在
紫
禁
城

IN THE FORBIDDEN CITY

China Institute
FOUNDED 1926

CnC 設計及文化研究工作室
DESIGN AND CULTURAL
STUDIES WORKSHOP

何 鴻 毅 家 族 基 金
THE ROBERT H. N. HO
FAMILY FOUNDATION

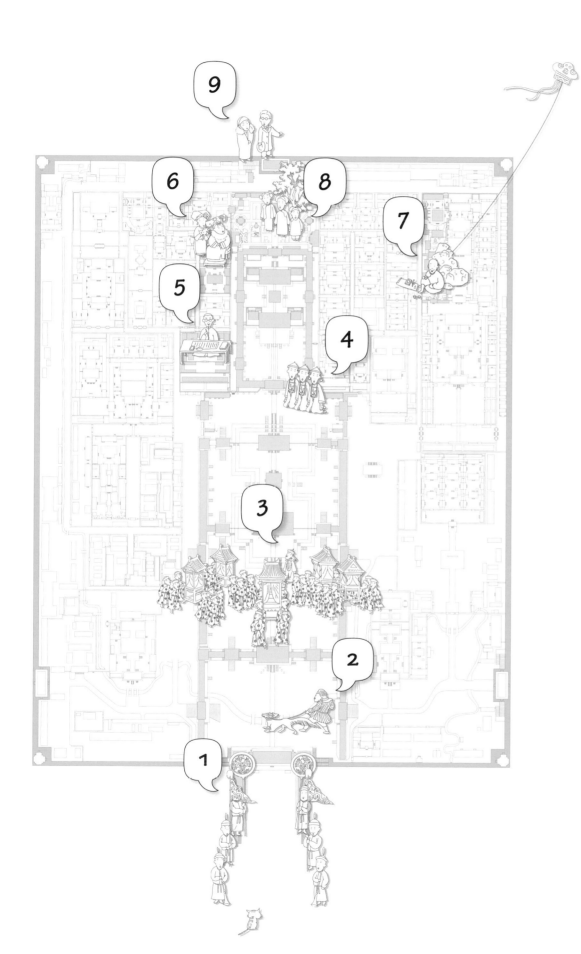

TABLE OF CONTENTS

The ancients believed that the star of *Ziwei*, also known as Polaris, never changed its position. They believed that the star was enclosed by a purple bright constellation and that it was the home of the Great Imperial Ruler of Heaven. In China, the emperor was thought to be the son of the Great Imperial Ruler of Heaven, and this was how his palace came to be called the Purple Forbidden City.

In 1421 the third Ming dynasty emperor, Yongle, working with the collective power of the nation, finished construction on this majestic palace in Beijing. The Forbidden City occupies a total area of 720,000 square meters. Flanking its four sides are colossal city walls and a broad palace moat. Together these protect a sprawling landscape of towers, halls, and pavilions, made up of red bricks and golden roof tiles.

For almost 600 years, the Forbidden City was the home of the Chinese emperor. It contained a stupendous amount of masterpieces and rare treasures, which were handed down from generation to generation. Countless imperial and historical events occurred here through the vicissitudes of time. Eventually, the Chinese Revolution of 1911 overthrew the imperial system that had ruled China for thousands of years. Then, in October of 1925, the Palace Museum was established on the grounds of the existing palace. On that day, the Forbidden City opened its doors to the public and, ever since, the palace has taken on the role of a spiritual home and cultural heritage site for everyone to enjoy.

Today, the Palace Museum is the world's largest and most well preserved royal architectural complex. Around 1,800,000 pieces of historical artifacts are stored inside. Every year, it welcomes tens of millions of visitors, as its allure and splendor increasingly attract greater attention from around the globe.

The Hong Kong-based scholar Mr. Chiu Kwong-chiu is someone who has planted his roots in the Forbidden City. He and his team, the Design and Cultural Studies Workshop, research and interpret the subject matter deeply and earnestly. Mr. Chiu's passion for the Forbidden City is evident in all of his books, from *The Grand Forbidden City – The Imperial Axis* to *The Twelve Beauties* to this current series, *We All Live in the Forbidden City*, which has been designed for a younger audience. Especially in this series of illustrative books, Mr. Chiu's unique perspective, along with the dynamic use of language and drawings, enliven and animate the Forbidden City, a place that is austere and lofty in nature. Through these books, you will experience the palace's grandeur, but you will also find delight in its refined elegance. In a joyful manner, everything that is unique about the Forbidden City comes to life.

It made me very happy to learn that the English editions of several books from *We All Live in the Forbidden City* would be published in New York. By way of these books, I hope that the children in North America will find themselves being transported on a colorful journey to the Forbidden City, as they develop their understanding of Chinese history and culture.

I wish everyone an exciting voyage!

Shan Jixiang
Director
The Palace Museum

When my father, Robert H. N. Ho, decided to establish a family foundation to support Chinese culture and Buddhist philosophy, it was a modest beginning to facing a formidable challenge: how to preserve and make more accessible globally the treasure trove which is embodied in over 5,000 years of Chinese history and culture. Since 2005, The Robert H. N. Ho Family Foundation, based in Hong Kong, has been active around the world, supporting cultural projects and academic exchange in collaboration with museums, galleries, universities, artists, curators, and scholars. Education has been a common thread running through all of our foundation's work, especially the development of cultural awareness amongst the emerging generation of young Chinese who, not unlike their counterparts around the world, have been swept away by the compelling amusements of the Internet and 21st century youth culture.

Chinese parents, like parents around the world, are concerned that their children might lose their connection with their cultural roots. It was with that in mind that our foundation decided to support Mr. Chiu Kwong-chiu and his team at Design and Cultural Studies Workshop in Hong Kong, to develop a series of books, *We All Live in the Forbidden City*, using the theme of Beijing's ancient palace as a platform to educate young people about many important aspects of Chinese history and culture. The books and related outreach activities have proved to be a popular and engaging way to inform as well as "edutain."

Having supported these publications both in Hong Kong (published in traditional Chinese characters) and in mainland China (published in simplified Chinese characters), it is only natural that we make these award-winning books more widely available to an English language audience. As urban areas in North America, Europe and the Antipodes become increasingly multi-cultural, so has our world become smaller with the increasing interdependence, economic and otherwise, between East and West. It is crucially important that young people learn more not just about their own culture, but also explore other cultures as well. My family and I hope this wonderful English language version, developed in collaboration with China Institute in America and Tuttle Publishing, will help bridge the gap between East and West, and continue to inform and entertain young people around the world.

Robert Yau Chung Ho
Chairman
The Robert H. N. Ho Family Foundation

BEFORE THE TOUR BEGINS:
ABOUT THE FORBIDDEN CITY

The Forbidden City became the epicenter of China's imperial empire after the third Ming Dynasty emperor, Yongle, relocated his court from Nanjing to Beijing. It took ten years to design the Forbidden City, but construction only lasted four years and the palace was completed in 1420. One hundred thousand craftsmen and over a million laborers were needed to build what is now the world's largest enclosed palace and the world's largest wooden architectural complex.

In imperial China the emperor was considered the "Son of Heaven" and the Forbidden City, as the focal point of the emperor's rule, was where "heaven" met "earth." Therefore every element of the Forbidden City was designed to serve a symbolic and ceremonial purpose for the imperial dynasties, dictating how the palace was used and how it projected power to the world. For example, the palace was designed along the Central Axis (also called the Imperial Path), which runs from the north to the south. According to the principles of feng shui, a long unbroken line contains devastating power. Through the use of the Central Axis, the imperial rulers were declaring that this power could only be harnessed by an emperor.

As the design of the Forbidden City projected an image of dynastic power to the world, it also dictated how daily life was conducted within. The palace was separated into two main sections: the Outer Court and the Inner Court. The Outer Court takes up the southern portion of the complex and was designed for the public life of the emperor. This is where court was held, imperial proclamations were delivered, and important ceremonies were conducted. The Inner Court to the north was for the emperor's private life and contained gardens, studies, and the empresses' chambers. Scholars, civil servants, and military men conducted their business in the Outer Court. Unless given special permission, only eunuchs, palace women, and children were allowed in the Inner Court. Even the emperor was not allowed in all of the rooms of the palace.

Since 1420, the Forbidden City has witnessed the triumphs, struggles, and shifting fortunes of Chinese history. After Emperor Yongle moved the capital to Beijing, the empire enjoyed a period of prosperity. The Great Wall as we see it today was constructed and China traded goods with countries from all over the world. Towards the end of the Ming dynasty, the emperors became more and more insulated and ineffectual and power became centered on the corrupt eunuchs that served as the emperors' advisors. Eventually rebellions broke out across China and the Ming Dynasty was overthrown. In 1644 Manchu invaders from the north established the Qing Dynasty.

Under the rule of Qing emperors Kangxi, Yongzheng, and Qianlong (lasting from 1662 to 1795) the Chinese kingdom became wealthy and powerful once again. In the 19th century, the empire suffered a slow decline, crippled by invasions from foreign countries and unsuccessful attempts at reform and modernization. Puyi, the last emperor of the Qing Dynasty, abdicated the throne in 1912. In the Republican Era that followed, a number of leaders and political factions fought for power. In 1925, the Forbidden City became the Palace Museum, open to the general public. The People's Republic of China, ruled by the Communist Party, was founded in 1949.

When you unfold this book you will travel through this history in strange and surprising ways. You will tour the Forbidden City from the Meridian Gate at the front to the Gate of Divine Prowess in the back, mingling with tourists from the present and emperors from the past all at once. The events that took place within the Forbidden City have too often been shrouded in mystery, but you will be joined by a mischievous cat, who is able to sneak through all the courtyards and over all of the palace walls, watching with you as history comes to life.

China Institute in America

FLYING EAGLE

HUNTING DOG

The Forbidden City was the home of the emperors of the Ming and Qing dynasties. It is said that during the golden days of the Ming dynasty, there were a staggering 100,000 eunuchs in the palace with 7,000 court maids to serve the emperor alone. It was very extravagant! By the Qing dynasty, however, the monarchs began to adopt a more austere and frugal way of living. The numbers of eunuchs and maids gradually decreased until there were only 100 to 200 people serving the last emperor. By then all the past excesses had disappeared under the great wheels of history.

Then the Qing dynasty fell and the palace became the Palace Museum. Now, every morning, tens of thousands of curious visitors set their feet on the "imperial paths" that were once reserved for emperors, exploring the grand palace where at one time tens of thousands of people played their parts in imperial life.

As there were many people in the palace, there were also many animals. Some of them were mythical animals, the most prominent being the dragon. They took up almost every important position inside the palace. Among the living animals, the crow was the most respected. It was able to fly freely above the palace.

Some animals had official duties. At the East Prosperity Gate there was a department with hunting dogs and eagles, which were kept so that the Manchu aristocracy could uphold the legendary lifestyle that their nomadic forefathers led north of China. There were also thoroughbred horses, which symbolized military prowess, and there were elephants stationed at important ceremonies to convey the authority and power of the emperor.

At one time during the Ming dynasty, there were crickets chirping throughout the Inner Court and the reckless Emperor Zhengde reared leopards during his reign. Toward the end of the Qing dynasty, it was rumored that the Empress Dowager Cixi had a pet monkey with the countenance and manners of a fawning slave. There were also cats in the Forbidden City, but they did not have any official duties or special status.

Although cats were not as favored as dogs, they were as free as the crows. Crows could fly freely in the sky while cats strolled leisurely on the beams and rooftops. Neither of them affected the course of history, but they witnessed every story that took place inside the palace walls…

I'VE WITNESSED...

ELEPHANTS THAT STOOD GUARD AT IMPORTANT CEREMONIES

THOROUGHBRED HORSES THAT SYMBOLIZED MILITARY PROWESS

CRICKETS COLLECTED BY THE ENTIRE NATION

QING DYNASTY DOGS

I'VE WITNESSED...

LITTLE CATS THAT HAD NO OFFICIAL DUTIES, BUT FULLY ENJOYED THEIR FREEDOM

CELESTIAL CROW

RED FRUIT

In a Manchurian myth, a celestial maiden conceived a child after
she ate a red fruit brought to her by a celestial crow. This
child became the founding ancestor of the Manchus.

THE GRAND PROCESSION
AS EMPEROR KANGXI
RETURNED TO THE PALACE

A CEREMONY WHERE
CAPTIVES ARE HANDED
OVER TO THE EMPEROR

A MING DYNASTY
MINISTER BEING LASHED
ON THE BUTTOCKS

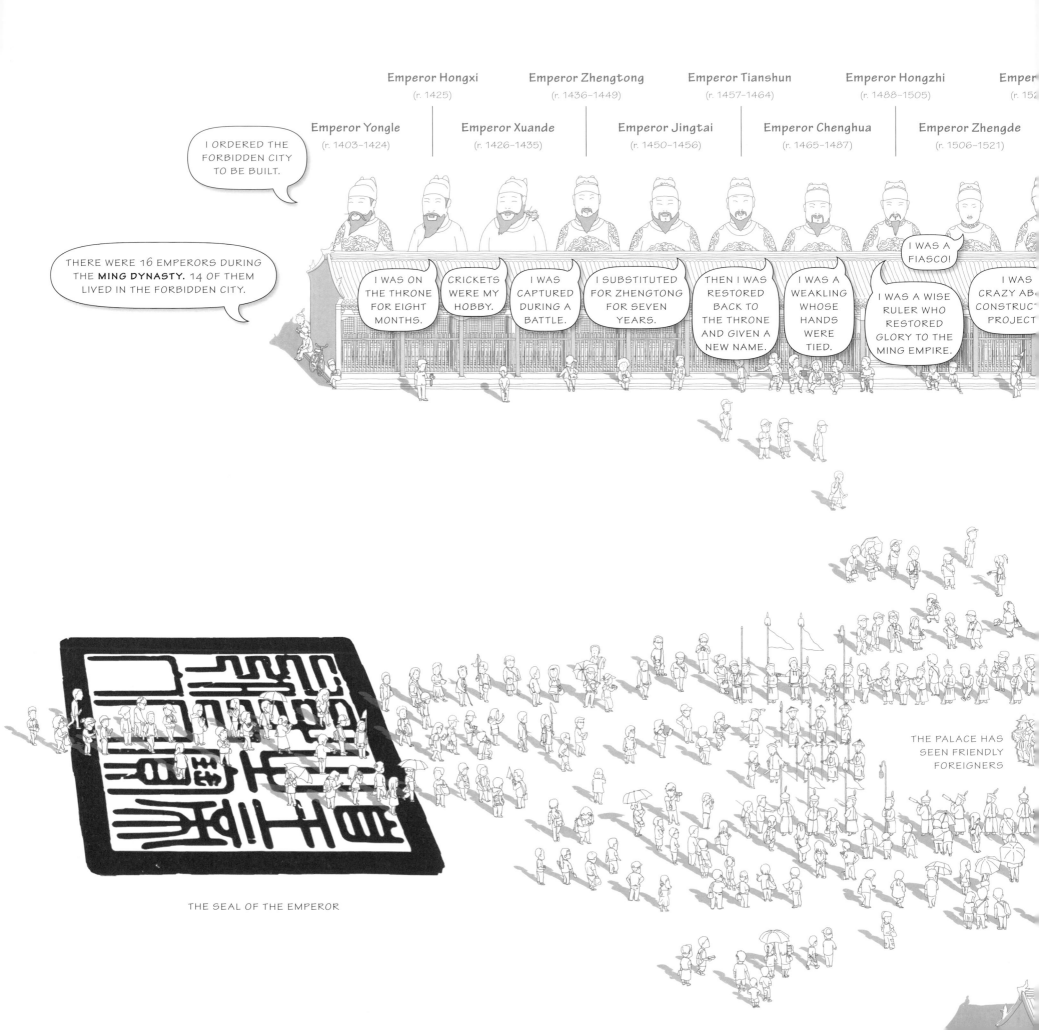

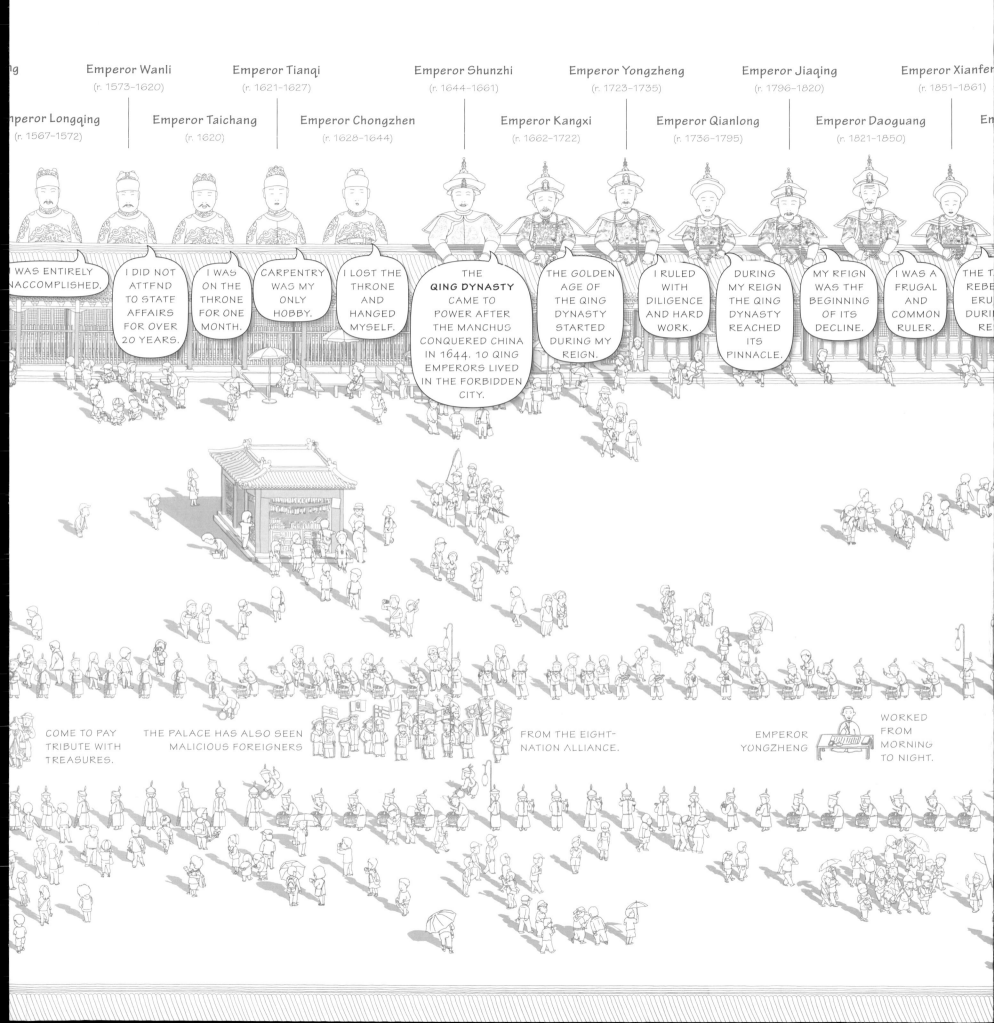

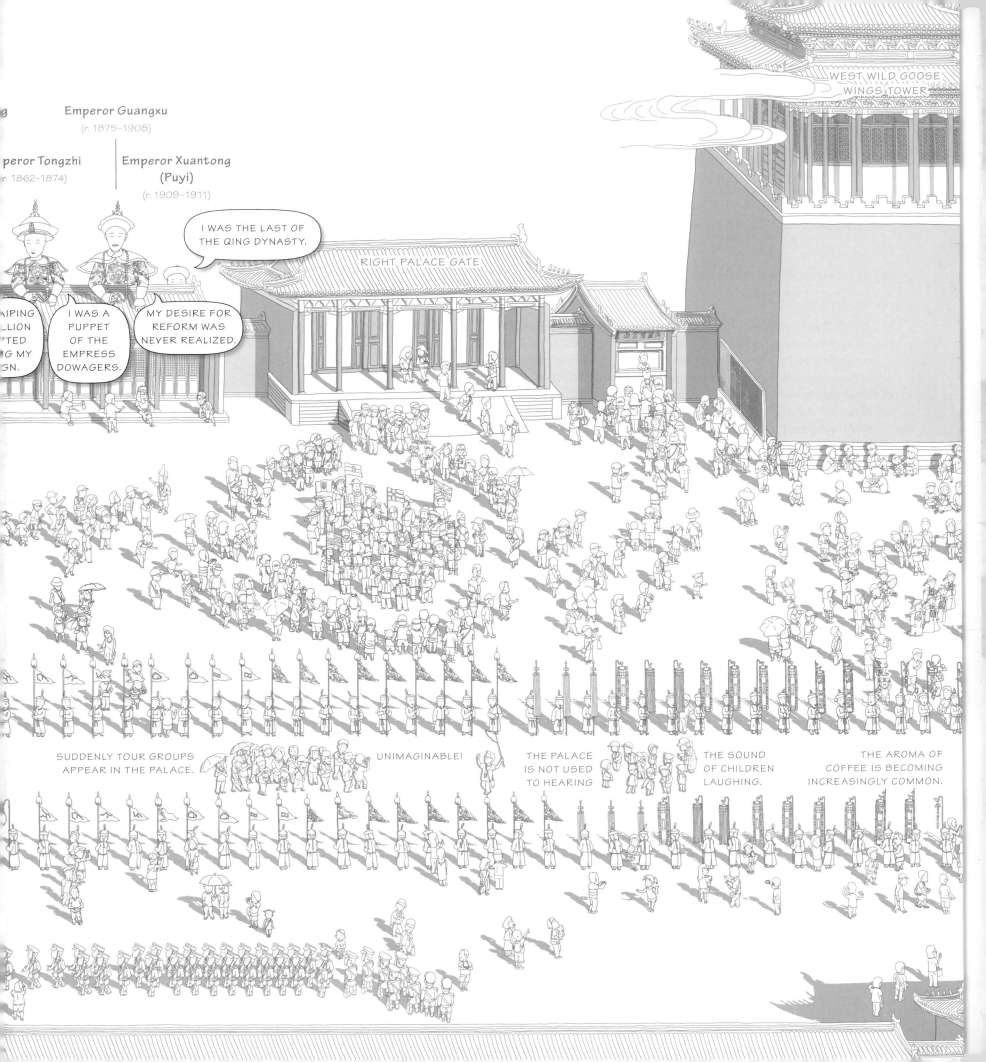

THE MERIDIAN GATE

In 1368, after the Ming army toppled the Mongols of the Yuan dynasty, a new dynasty was founded that returned China to native Han rule. During the Ming dynasty, the stupendous Great Wall and magnificent imperial tombs were constructed, Emperor Yongle dispatched the largest fleet of ships in the world to seas that the Chinese had never explored before, and the city of Beijing was one of the world's grandest metropolises. It was during these golden years that the timeless Forbidden City was erected.

Facing south, the Meridian Gate is the front gate of the Forbidden City, the entrance to the palace that was the center of the universe for the Ming and Qing dynasties.

At the Meridian Gate the imperial almanac was issued to the Chinese people, foreign envoys came to pay tribute to the imperial family, the newly pronounced top three scholars of the imperial examination made their triumphal exit, and prisoners of war, down on their knees, were examined by the emperor. During the Ming dynasty, ministers and vassals gathered here before dawn to wait for the emperor to hold court. It was here, in the halcyon days of the Qing dynasty, that Emperor Kangxi set out on his famed inspection tour to the south. It was through here, in the twilight years of the Qing dynasty, that soldiers from the Eight-Nation Alliance forced their way into the palace.

The Meridian Gate leads into the Forbidden City, the former home of the imperial family. The political and personal affairs that took place here were equally momentous during the history of the Ming and Qing dynasties.

MERIDIAN GATE

PUYI IS RIDING HIS BICYCLE AGAIN.

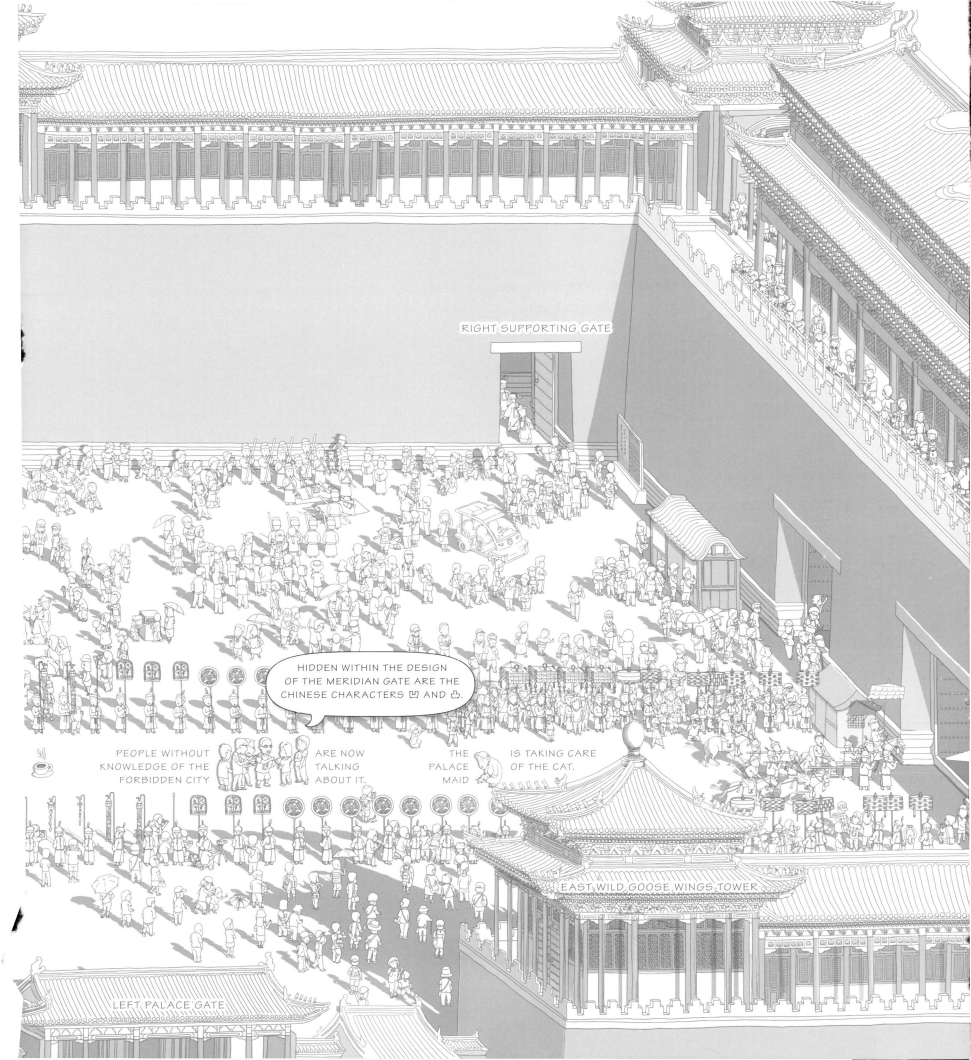

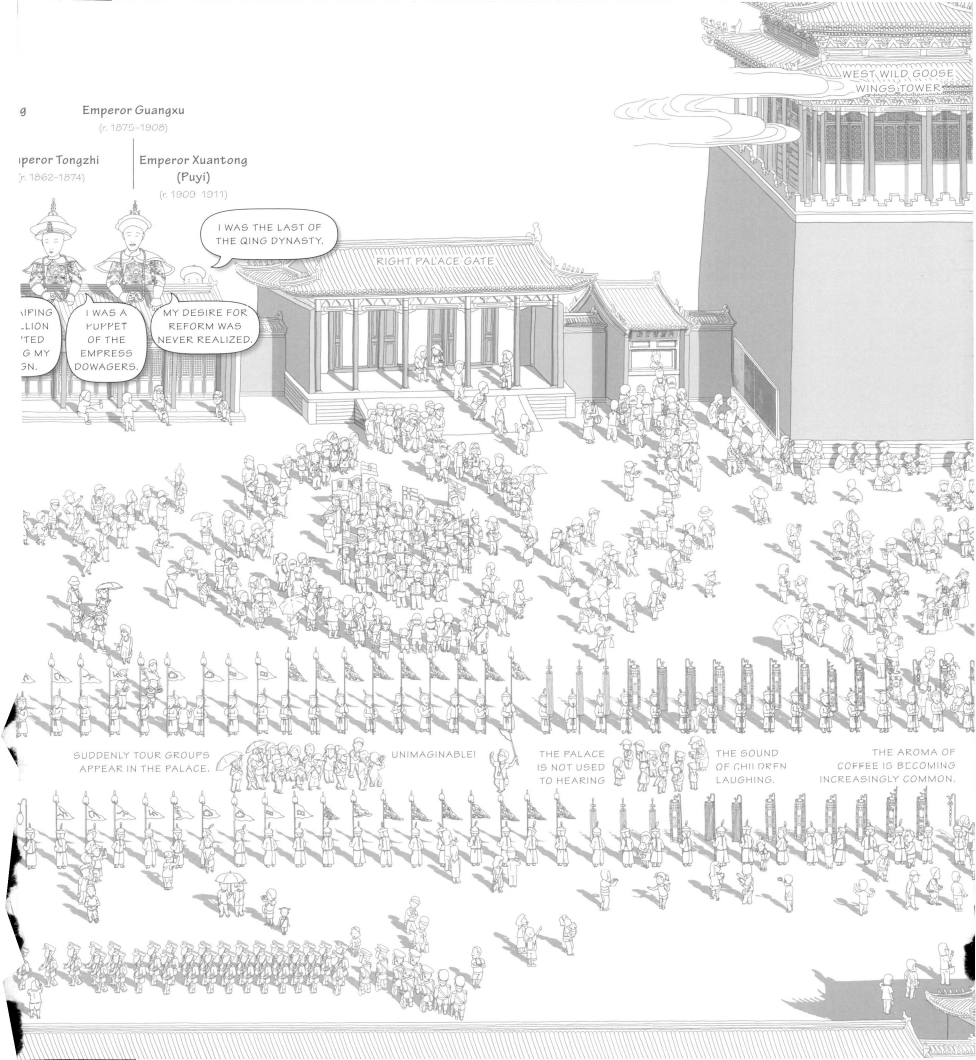

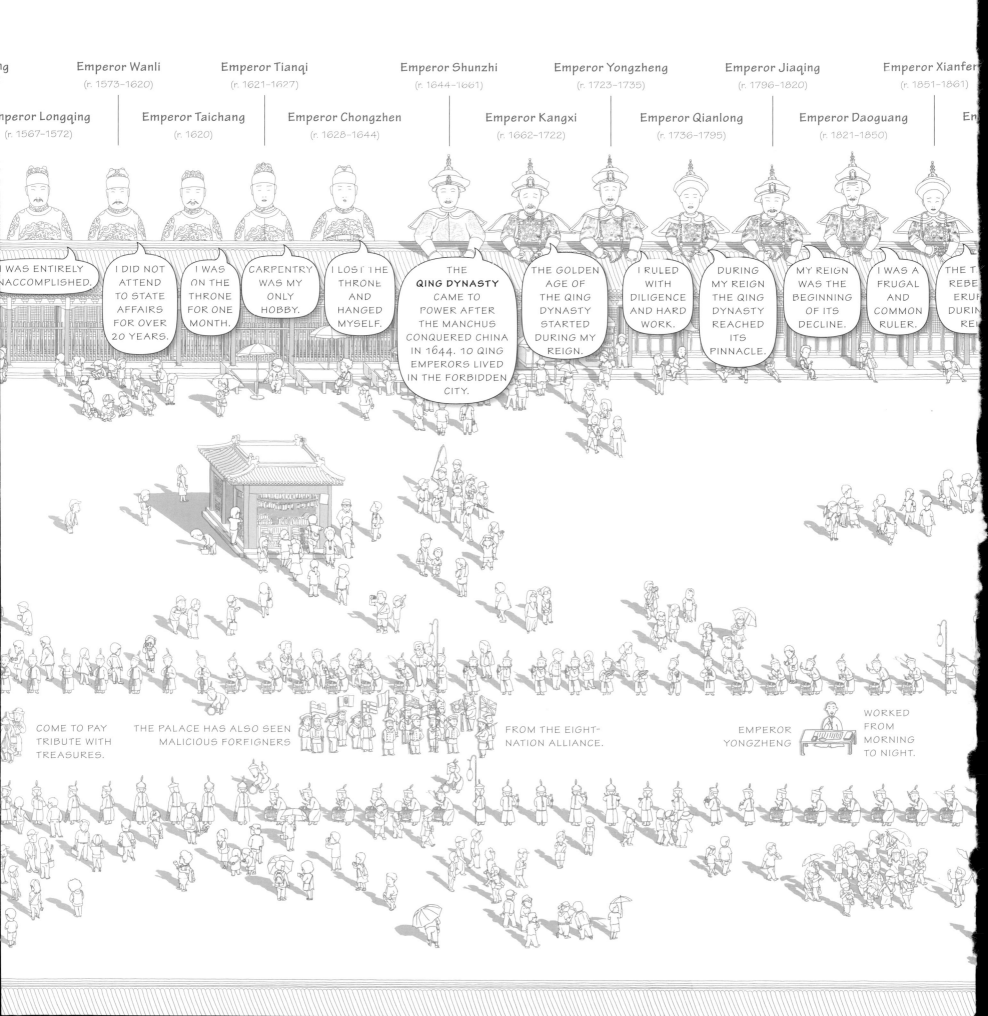

THE YEAR TEN THOUSAND ENVOYS CAME TO PAY TRIBUTE

The year 1761 marked the 50th birthday of Emperor Qianlong and the 70th birthday of his mother, the Empress Dowager.

That same year construction of the Tower of Purple Light was completed and portraits were painted of the most outstanding officials. To celebrate, an imperial banquet was held for them, along with other ministers, generals, and Mongolian princes.

That year *The History of the Palace*, commissioned by Emperor Qianlong, was also completed.

The year before, 1760, the 15th royal prince Yongyan (the future Emperor Jiaqing) was born in *Yuanmingyuan*, a residential palace (also called the Old Summer Palace) on the outskirts of Beijing.

This same year the Qing dynasty put down insurgencies by the Dzungars and Muslim tribes in Western China, completing an important mission to expand the empire's borders.

The year 1761 was the year that ten thousand envoys came to pay tribute.

← *To the Hall of Martial Valor*

GATE OF GLORIOUS HARMONY

RIVER OF GOLDEN WATER

This scene is based on a famous scroll painting titled *Ten Thousand Envoys Come to Pay Tribute*. The painting was made using a bird's-eye view, looking down at the Inner Golden Water Bridges from a Meridian Gate tower. It portrays a glorious historic moment in the Qing dynasty: envoys from foreign countries and Qing empire colonies passing through the Gate of Supreme Harmony to pay respect and tribute to the emperor.

In the preface of *Chronicles of the Great Qing Dynasty*, it says, "There were 57 colonies of China and 31 foreign countries at the time that came to pay tribute."

The painting *Ten Thousand Envoys Come to Pay Tribute* shows emissaries coming to the Chinese court from Asian and European countries, including Joseon, Brunei, Vietnam, the Lao Kingdoms, Cambodia, Siam, Malacca, Songkhla, Johor, Luzon, the Kingdom of Great Britain, Russia, Holland, France, Portugal, Bologna, Galaba, Kuqa, the Kingdom of Hungary, and many others.

It shows the envoys holding their national flags with Chinese words on them and carrying treasures and exotic animals. They are waiting in line to be granted an audience with the Chinese emperor. As the number of envoys was tremendous,

the site was overflowing with bustling crowds and palace officials had to assign special staff members to maintain calm and order.

This scroll was one in a series of paintings by anonymous court painters. It should be noted that there were no trees in the courtyard at the time. Some claim this is because a treeless plain would highlight the somberness and grandeur of the imperial court. Others claim this is because the trees are wood. In the Chinese cosmology of the five elements, wood is believed to have a negative effect on earth – the symbol of the imperial force of the emperor. Therefore, the imperial rulers

would not want any living trees around the focal point of their power. In any case, the trees in this painting were added randomly.

Mistakes in such paintings could also be made because the court painters were not allowed to witness such ceremonial activities. So their paintings were based on descriptions by others who had been there, by written records, or by similar paintings from the past.

The painter also incorrectly placed the pair of bronze lions in front of the Gate of Supreme Harmony so that the male lion playing with a ball was on the right and the female lion tending her cub was on the left. This mistake has been corrected in this drawing.

There are other inaccuracies, such as some missing bronze urns. Judging by the enthusiastic signed inscription by Emperor Qianlong, perhaps he was not bothered by miscellaneous details so long as the painting had fulfilled its purpose of recording the grand event.

In 1757, Emperor Qianlong started his second imperial inspection tour in southern China, to examine the waterworks and irrigation systems, as well as the safety and well-being of the people.

In 1762, Emperor Qianlong embarked on his third imperial inspection tour to the south. Tremendous and stupendous expenses were lavished on every single stage of the journey, in spite of the pronouncement in his imperial edict that "excessive extravagance in all affairs must be avoided."

THE LAST GRAND WEDDING CEREMONY

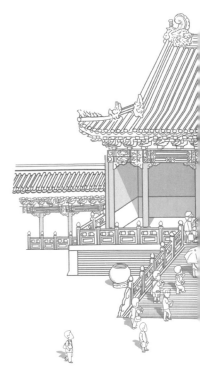

In olden times, most people got married at an early age, often between the ages of 13 and 17. Because most emperors got married when they were still young princes, there were few royal wedding ceremonies held in the palace for reigning emperors.

The wedding ceremony of Emperor Guangxu was held in 1889, on the 27th day of the first lunar month. Guangxu turned 19 that year, generally considered "past the proper age to be married." It was believed that by putting off the marriage, his aunt, Empress Dowager Cixi, was trying to delay Guangxu from becoming the real and executive emperor. She had been appointed his regent, to rule in his name until his wedding day.

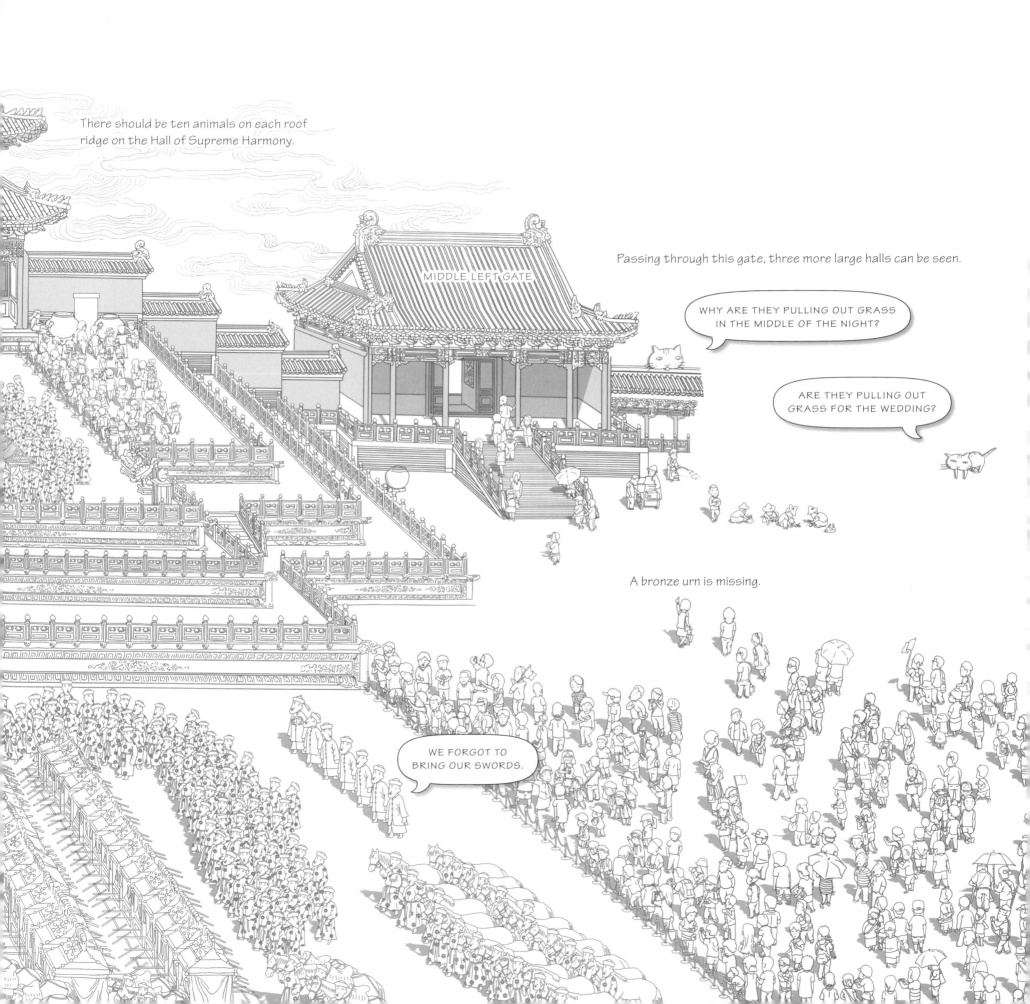

Before the wedding ceremony Empress Dowager Cixi, following precedents of the royal court, issued an edict that said, "Austerity and frugality must be exercised in matters of man-power and monetary expenses as regards the ceremony, while extravagance and excess must be avoided in all affairs." Quite to the contrary, however, it ended up being one of the most lavish royal weddings in the history of China. The expenses totaled an astounding 5,500,000 silver taels, which was about a quarter of all the silver in the national treasury. The silver spent on the wedding ceremony could have bought 4,000,000 *dan* of grain, sufficient to feed 22,800,000 people for a month. Guangxu was the last emperor of the Qing dynasty to have such an enormous amount of money spent on his wedding. It was beyond enough!

The wedding ceremony, which was held at the auspicious moment of midnight, is depicted in this drawing of a painting from the album *The Wedding Ceremony of the Guangxu Emperor*. The entire wedding lasted for 104 days! The grandeur of the wedding was in fact an attempt to project power at a time when China faced threats of invasion by foreign forces and when the Qing monarchy was declining in strength and reputation.

More than 90 paintings were produced for the royal wedding album. Emperor Guangxu seems to appear in only two of them. In both of them he is kneeling with his back to the painters, paying high respect to Empress Dowager Cixi.

EMPEROR GUANGXU
IN *PORTRAITS OF
GREETINGS IN RESPECT*

EMPEROR GUANGXU IN
PORTRAITS OF ETIQUETTE

One More Tale: A Serious Fire at the Gate of Supreme Harmony

At the Gate of Supreme Harmony, where ten thousand envoys paid tribute to Emperor Qianlong, there was a serious fire that broke out 40 days before the royal wedding. This happened during the depths of winter and the River of Golden Water was frozen over. So the palace staff had to resort to digging through the ice to get water to put out the fire. As the fire lasted for two whole days, the houses to the east and the west of the Gate of Supreme Harmony – including the warehouses where the wardrobes, equipment, decorations, and utensils for the wedding were stored – burned down to the ground. After the fire was finally extinguished, the 7,000 people in the rescue force were rewarded a large compensation for their relief efforts… yet another big expense.

The Gate of Supreme Harmony that we see today was rebuilt after the fire. For the construction of the restored Gate of Supreme Harmony, the Bureau of Construction submitted a budget of expenses that totaled 235,000 silver taels. This means Emperor Guangxu's wedding ceremony cost the equivalent of building 23 Gates of Supreme Harmony, with money left over!

Labels on illustration:

MIDDLE LEFT GATE

REAR LEFT GATE

GATE OF GOOD FORTUNE

Speech bubbles:

IT'S VERY TIGHT

FOREIGN ENVOYS BARGE RUDELY INTO THE INNER COURT WITHOUT PERMISSION.

HERE IS WHERE OFFICIALS AND SERVICE STAFF WAIT FOR THE ANNOUNCEMENT OF THE EMPEROR'S ARRIVAL.

BETWEEN HOME AND COUNTRY

In imperial China a palace was called "The Great Within." The Forbidden City's Three Great Palaces of the Outer Court – the Hall of Supreme Harmony, the Hall of Central Harmony, and the Hall of Preserving Harmony – are separated from the Inner Court by a 1.6 kilometer long red wall. These back palaces are "the great within within the Great Within" and were the most secretive quarters in the palace.

The Gate of Heavenly Purity leading to the Inner Court sits behind the Hall of Preserving Harmony. The square in front of it is long and narrow, measuring 200 meters long and ranging from 50 meters to 30 meters wide at its narrowest section.

The back palaces are lower than the Three Great Halls. If one stands on the 8-meter high platform in the back of the Hall of Preserving Harmony, you will feel like you are seeing the whole Inner Court spread out in front of you. But your vision is limited and you will not see beyond the golden tiles on the rooftops. This is because the narrow 30-meter distance does not give you enough space to look down and into the Inner Court. Due to these clever designs, the privacy of the Inner Court was maintained.

Throughout the Qing dynasty, the emperors held official court in front of the Gate of Heavenly Purity and slept behind it. In other words, the Gate of Heavenly Purity is where the line was drawn between public and private state affairs for the emperors. Without special permission from the emperor, not even high ministers would ever be able to cross it.

The Hall of Heavenly Purity, the most prominent of the Three Back Palaces, served as the imperial living quarters for 15 emperors during the Ming and Qing dynasties. Though Emperor Kangxi was the last emperor who lived there, it retained its significance as the hall where the emperor's body was laid in state before being laid to rest.

The Hall of Heavenly Purity was not used to receive ministers during the Ming dynasty. Therefore, for a long time, what actually happened here was a mystery. A biography of Ming dynasty emperors includes the following description: "[in the Hall of Heavenly Purity] there were 27 beds that provided the emperor with different places to nap wherever and whenever he felt like. It is extremely unusual." Yes, it was a strange set-up, and even the eunuchs did not know where His Majesty was from one night to the next. This ingenious game of hide-and-seek was for the emperor's security and safety, but perhaps it did not ensure a good-night's sleep as bizarre incidents repeatedly took place here.

When Emperor Yongzheng moved his living quarters to the Hall of Mental Cultivation in the early 1700s, the Hall of Heavenly Purity became the location where the emperor tended to affairs of state and received foreign envoys. It was used for rituals and banquets on festivals and holidays, including New Year's Day, the Dragon Boat Festival, and the Mid-Autumn Festival.

There are two fabled objects in the Hall of Heavenly Purity: a famous plaque with an engraving that reads "Upright and Pure in Mind," which was hung in the front hall of the palace, and the even more famous "Box with the Name of the Heir Apparent." These items might look unassuming, but there is a remarkable story as to how they got here.

GATE OF LUNAR ESSENCE

HALL OF HEAVENLY PURITY

GATE OF SOLAR ESSENCE

THE GREAT WITHIN

Emperor Yongzheng had been involved in a fierce and bloody struggle with his fellow princes to claim themselves as the legitimate heir to his father and predecessor, Emperor Kangxi. He came up with an unprecedented method to prevent this from happening again. The emperor was to secretly issue two copies of an imperial edict that would name his heir apparent. One copy was to be carried by the emperor at all times and the other was to be placed inside the "Box with the Name of the Heir Apparent," which was hidden behind the "Upright and Pure in Mind" plaque.

In the event of the death of the emperor, a group of the most trusted officials would take out the copy in the "Box with the Name of the Heir Apparent" in front of ministers and members of the royal family. This copy would be matched with the one taken from the inner layers of the clothes on the deceased emperor. The name on the two imperial edicts would then be announced as the proper heir.

As all of this was carried out with upright and pure intentions, the problem of succession to the throne was solved with limited struggle through the rest of the Qing dynasty. Four emperors succeeded the throne using this system: Qianlong, Jiaqing, Daoguang, and Xianfeng. Emperor Xianfeng's only son, Emperor Tongzhi, had no heir. From this point on Empress Dowager Cixi had the power to appoint the emperor.

YIN AND YANG: HEAVEN AND EARTH

PALACE OF EARTHLY TRANQUILITY

HALL OF UNION

HALL OF HEAVENLY PURITY

GATE OF HEAVENLY PURITY

OFFICE OF THE GRAND COUNCIL OF STATE

SOUTH WAREHOUSE

IMPERIAL KITCHENS

INNER OFFICE FOR REPORTING STATE AFFAIRS

GATE OF LUNAR ESSENCE

MOUNT FOR PALANQUINS

OFFICE FOR ENDORSING DOCUMENTS

This way to the Hall of Mental Cultivation

This way to the Hall of Heavenly Purity

Holding court, the emperor sat on the imperial throne in the center of the gate. The managing ministers stood to the east and the west of the throne, while the reporting ministers knelt below the eastern steps. They then took turns presenting their reports to the emperor. With regular affairs, the emperor would deliver his edicts immediately; for especially urgent or grave matters, the emperor would dismiss all but the most essential ministers. While still kneeling these ministers would move up the steps to be near the emperor for a consultation. When a decision was reached or a policy was made, an imperial edict would be issued quickly and efficiently.

Emperor Kangxi was the most diligent emperor of the Qing dynasty. He almost never missed holding court during his long reign of 60 years. His was the first of the Qing dynasty's three most brilliant and successful reigns: Kangxi, Yongzheng, and Qianlong. A gradual decline followed this golden age until the emperors stopped holding official court altogether after Emperor Xianfeng's reign ended in 1861.

When the court was moved from the Gate of Supreme Harmony to the Gate of Heavenly Purity, it cut the distance between the emperor's living quarters and the site where court was held from 1,000 meters to a walking distance of less than 50 steps.

Let us think about how this might have affected the emperors. The first and second Ming emperors sometimes held court three times a day. If the late Ming emperor Wanli had been as diligent as they were, he would have walked more than 7,200 kilometers going back and forth to court, or about the entire length of the Great Wall of China! But the lazy Emperor Wanli did not hold court for over 20 years and left his royal duties to corrupt eunuchs, causing the imperial family to lose control of power. Could this mean that the distance between the emperor's private quarters and the court led to the decline and eventual end of the Ming dynasty?

During the Qing dynasty, on the other hand, power was centralized near the emperor's private quarters. This allowed the Qing to be strong and prosperous in the early years, but later led to an autocratic, insulated mentality that weakened the government and exposed it to repeated misfortunes. This, too, might have had something to do with where emperors held court!

The emperors moved their daily court from the Gate of Supreme Harmony to the Gate of Heavenly Purity during the early years of the Qing dynasty.

The time of day when the emperors held court differed based on the seasons. During the winter the emperors mercifully ordered the morning court to start later, at 8:00 a.m., since the high ministers would have had to travel in total darkness to report to an earlier court. The Qing emperors were also so kind to some elderly ministers as to let them ride on horseback or take a palanquin to court.

When reporting to court the ministers would enter the palace either through the East Prosperity Gate (the east gate to the palace) and arrive at the Archery Pavilion, or they would pass through the West Prosperity Gate (the west gate to the palace) and arrive in front of the Imperial Household Department. From this point all had to walk to the Gate of Heavenly Purity.

The emperor's living quarters were located in the Hall of Heavenly Purity, positioned closely to where he dealt with affairs of the country. The princes were educated in the imperial study nearby. So while tending to the affairs of the nation, the emperor was able to enjoy the sound of his sons reciting the Chinese classics.

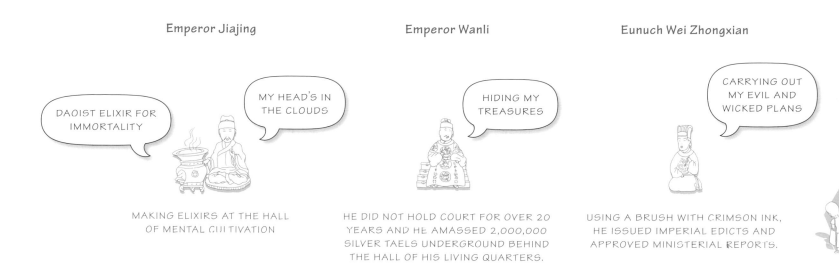

Emperor Jiajing

DAOIST ELIXIR FOR IMMORTALITY

MY HEAD'S IN THE CLOUDS

MAKING ELIXIRS AT THE HALL OF MENTAL CULTIVATION

Emperor Wanli

HIDING MY TREASURES

HE DID NOT HOLD COURT FOR OVER 20 YEARS AND HE AMASSED 2,000,000 SILVER TAELS UNDERGROUND BEHIND THE HALL OF HIS LIVING QUARTERS.

Eunuch Wei Zhongxian

CARRYING OUT MY EVIL AND WICKED PLANS

USING A BRUSH WITH CRIMSON INK, HE ISSUED IMPERIAL EDICTS AND APPROVED MINISTERIAL REPORTS.

All the emperors from the middle until the end of the Ming dynasty were notoriously incompetent. Emperor Jiajing's only passion was for making Daoist elixirs and in the process he turned the Inner Court into a large furnace for making these tonics. His all-around evil ways led to a rebellion and assassination attempt organized by the palace women. Scared out of his wits, Jiajing fled the Forbidden City.

Emperor Wanli was so crazed with greed that he buried a huge amount of silver behind the Hall of Mental Cultivation. Later, all of it was stolen by his eunuchs. How outlandish! Even worse, Wanli's negligence of state affairs planted a poisonous seed that led to the tragic end of the Ming dynasty. Without competent rulers, corrupt eunuchs seized state power. Concerning the Hall of Mental Cultivation, there weren't many records kept of what took place during this time period, because there wasn't much good to record.

HALL OF MENTAL CULTIVATION

"TO NOURISH THE MIND THERE IS NOTHING BETTER THAN TO MAKE ONE'S DESIRES FEW."
—MENCIUS

CENTRAL HALL

PLUM
GARDEN

EAST WARMT

CONFERENCE ROOM

THE ROOM OF
THREE RARITIES

HISTORY COMES TO LIFE

THE QING DYNASTY

BER — THE ROOM OF BEING AT EASE

Emperor Shunzhi

SMALLPOX

SHUNZHI DIED OF SMALLPOX IN THE HALL OF MENTAL CULTIVATION.

Emperor Kangxi

STUDYING HARD

THE HALL WAS USED AS A PALACE WORKSHOP DURING HIS REIGN.

Emperor Yongzheng

BLURRY VISION

EMPEROR YONGZHENG MOVED HIS LIVING QUARTERS HERE.

During the Golden Age of the Qing dynasty, Emperor Yongzheng moved his living quarters from the Hall of Heavenly Purity to the Hall of Mental Cultivation. At this time China's power knew few boundaries. For example, imperial edicts sent out as special deliveries by the Office of the Grand Council of State could travel as far as 600 or 800 *li* in one day. (1 *li* is about 1/2 of a kilometer.)

The years of peace and prosperity continued. Yongzheng's successor, Emperor Qianlong, retired after 60 years on the throne, naming his son Jiaqing as the next emperor. But he was still so influential that the Qianlong "era" continued for the next four years until his death.

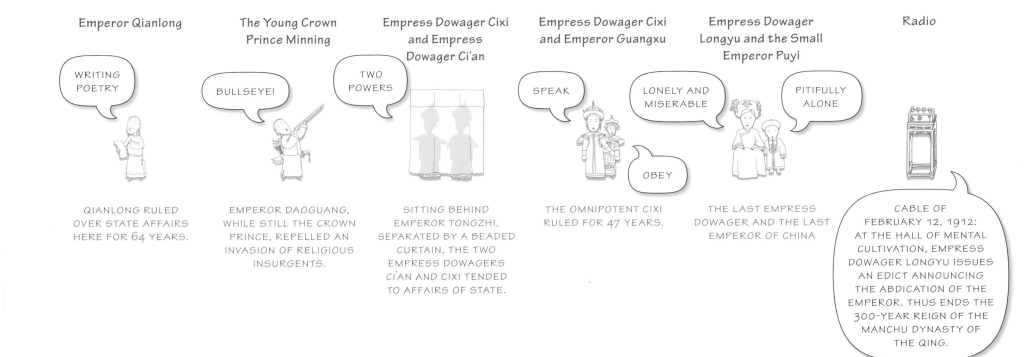

Emperor Qianlong

WRITING POETRY

QIANLONG RULED OVER STATE AFFAIRS HERE FOR 64 YEARS.

The Young Crown Prince Minning

BULLSEYE!

EMPEROR DAOGUANG, WHILE STILL THE CROWN PRINCE, REPELLED AN INVASION OF RELIGIOUS INSURGENTS.

Empress Dowager Cixi and Empress Dowager Ci'an

TWO POWERS

SITTING BEHIND EMPEROR TONGZHI, SEPARATED BY A BEADED CURTAIN, THE TWO EMPRESS DOWAGERS CI'AN AND CIXI TENDED TO AFFAIRS OF STATE.

Empress Dowager Cixi and Emperor Guangxu

SPEAK

OBEY

THE OMNIPOTENT CIXI RULED FOR 47 YEARS.

Empress Dowager Longyu and the Small Emperor Puyi

LONELY AND MISERABLE

PITIFULLY ALONE

THE LAST EMPRESS DOWAGER AND THE LAST EMPEROR OF CHINA

Radio

CABLE OF FEBRUARY 12, 1912: AT THE HALL OF MENTAL CULTIVATION, EMPRESS DOWAGER LONGYU ISSUES AN EDICT ANNOUNCING THE ABDICATION OF THE EMPEROR. THUS ENDS THE 300-YEAR REIGN OF THE MANCHU DYNASTY OF THE QING.

During his reign, Qianlong enjoyed more respect, good fortune, and longevity than most emperors in Chinese history. His elegant and scholarly study has been well preserved to this day, largely due to his lofty status as a wise and efficient ruler. None of the rulers that succeeded him had the capability or drive to reform or develop the ruling system.

After Qianlong's reign, the Qing dynasty and the imperial way of life slowly faded and declined. By the reign of Puyi, the last emperor, the Hall of Mental Cultivation was dilapidated and filled with miscellaneous goods.

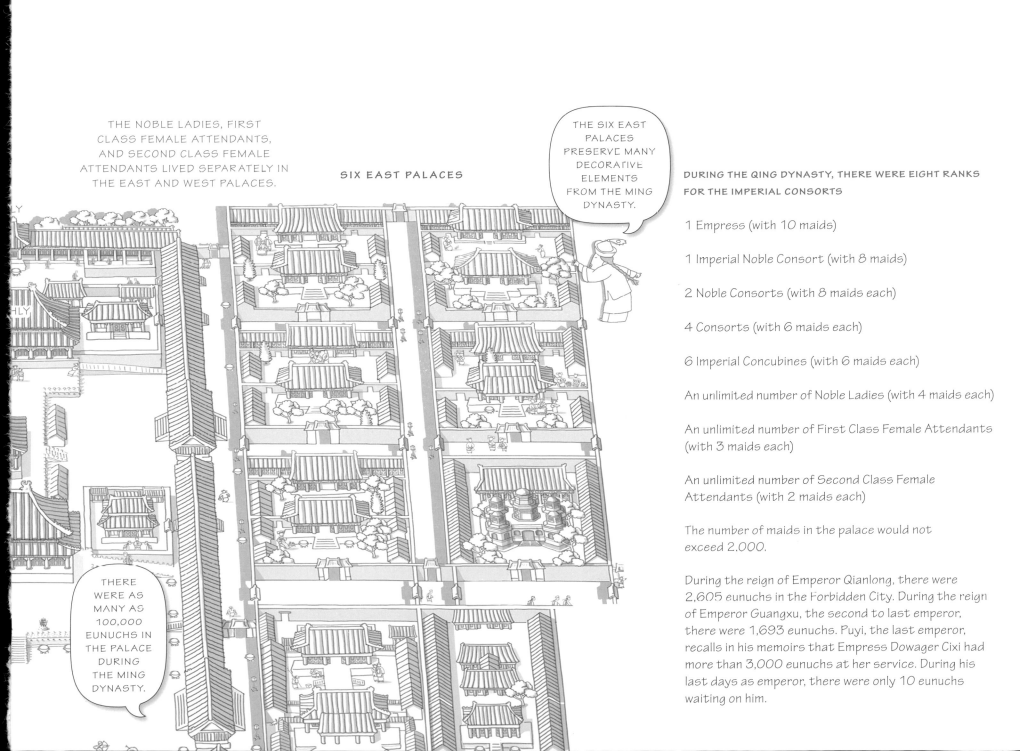

THE NOBLE LADIES, FIRST CLASS FEMALE ATTENDANTS, AND SECOND CLASS FEMALE ATTENDANTS LIVED SEPARATELY IN THE EAST AND WEST PALACES.

SIX EAST PALACES

THE SIX EAST PALACES PRESERVE MANY DECORATIVE ELEMENTS FROM THE MING DYNASTY.

THERE WERE AS MANY AS 100,000 EUNUCHS IN THE PALACE DURING THE MING DYNASTY.

DURING THE QING DYNASTY, THERE WERE EIGHT RANKS FOR THE IMPERIAL CONSORTS

1 Empress (with 10 maids)

1 Imperial Noble Consort (with 8 maids)

2 Noble Consorts (with 8 maids each)

4 Consorts (with 6 maids each)

6 Imperial Concubines (with 6 maids each)

An unlimited number of Noble Ladies (with 4 maids each)

An unlimited number of First Class Female Attendants (with 3 maids each)

An unlimited number of Second Class Female Attendants (with 2 maids each)

The number of maids in the palace would not exceed 2,000.

During the reign of Emperor Qianlong, there were 2,605 eunuchs in the Forbidden City. During the reign of Emperor Guangxu, the second to last emperor, there were 1,693 eunuchs. Puyi, the last emperor, recalls in his memoirs that Empress Dowager Cixi had more than 3,000 eunuchs at her service. During his last days as emperor, there were only 10 eunuchs waiting on him.

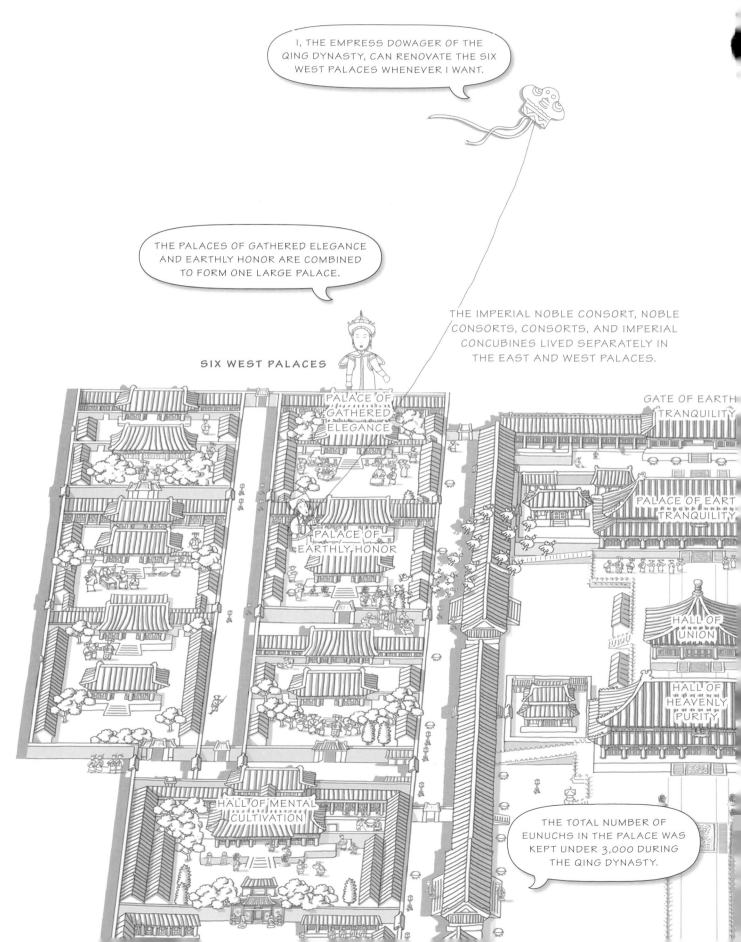

I, THE EMPRESS DOWAGER OF THE QING DYNASTY, CAN RENOVATE THE SIX WEST PALACES WHENEVER I WANT.

THE PALACES OF GATHERED ELEGANCE AND EARTHLY HONOR ARE COMBINED TO FORM ONE LARGE PALACE.

THE IMPERIAL NOBLE CONSORT, NOBLE CONSORTS, CONSORTS, AND IMPERIAL CONCUBINES LIVED SEPARATELY IN THE EAST AND WEST PALACES.

SIX WEST PALACES

PALACE OF GATHERED ELEGANCE

GATE OF EARTH TRANQUILITY

As the emperors lived in the Hall of Heavenly Purity, the empresses lived in the Palace of Earthly Tranquility behind it. When Emperor Yongzheng of the Qing dynasty moved his quarters to the Hall of Mental Cultivation, the empress moved as well. The Palace of Earthly Tranquility was then used for weddings and Manchu ritual ceremonies. The empress and imperial consorts then took residence in the Six East Palaces and the Six West Palaces. Each of these palaces were designed in traditional Chinese architectural style, 50 meters in length and width, with courtyards, a main hall, and houses on three sides.

PALACE OF EARTHLY HONOR

PALACE OF EART TRANQUILITY

HALL OF UNION

HALL OF HEAVENLY PURITY

HALL OF MENTAL CULTIVATION

WITH HOUSES ONLY ON THREE SIDES, THESE PALACES LOOK LIKE THE OFFICES THAT ARE ALWAYS OPEN FOR DUTY!

THE TOTAL NUMBER OF EUNUCHS IN THE PALACE WAS KEPT UNDER 3,000 DURING THE QING DYNASTY.

EMPRESS DOWAGER CIXI

I LOVE ORCHIDS.

SHE ENTERS THE PALACE.

A MEMBER OF THE MANCHU YEHENARA CLAN, CIXI (1835–1908) WAS NAMED ALMOND AS A CHILD. WHEN SHE BECAME A STUDENT SHE WAS NAMED XINGZHEN. IT WAS ALSO SAID THAT HER NAME WAS LITTLE ORCHID.

SHE IS OFTEN ADDRESSED AS NOBLE LADY ORCHID.

IN TEN YEARS, SHE WAS PROMOTED SIX LEVELS. SHE ROSE FROM A NOBLE LADY TO EMPRESS DOWAGER.

HE'S THE FUTURE EMPEROR TONGZHI.

SHE ENTERS THE PALACE OF GATHERED ELEGANCE.

SHE'S EXPECTING!

15 YEARS OLD (1851)   She is selected as a consort and given the title of Noble Lady Lan.

19 YEARS OLD (1854)   Promoted to Imperial Concubine Yi.

21 YEARS OLD (1856)   Gives birth to Crown Prince Zaichun; immediately promoted to Consort Yi.

22 YEARS OLD (1857)   Promoted to Noble Consort Yi.

25 YEARS OLD (1860)   After the allied forces of England and France invade and take Beijing she flees with Emperor Xianfeng to the Mountain Resort in Chengde.

26 YEARS OLD (1861)   When Emperor Xianfeng passes away, her son becomes Emperor Tongzhi, and she is promoted to Empress Dowager. With her son too young to rule, she successfully orchestrates a coup over powerful ministers and is appointed co-regent with the Empress Dowager Ci'an. Sitting behind Emperor Tongzhi, separated by a beaded curtain, the two empress dowagers tend to affairs of state.

EMPRESS DOWAGER

SHE RETURNS TO THE PALACE OF GATHERED ELEGANCE.

27 YEARS OLD (1862)   She is given the name Cixi.

39 YEARS OLD (1874)   Emperor Tongzhi passes away and is succeeded by Cixi's nephew Emperor Guangxu.

50 YEARS OLD (1884)   Celebrating her 50th birthday, Cixi returns to the Palace of Gathered Elegance from the Palace of Eternal Spring, spending 630,000 silver taels on renovations.

53 YEARS OLD (1888)   Emperor Guangxu marries and the following year takes over state affairs. Although she is officially retired, Cixi continues her "political tutelage."

IT'S AN EXTRAVAGANT PALACE.

59 YEARS OLD (1894)   For her 60th birthday celebration, Cixi spends lavishly to reconstruct and enlarge the Summer Palace, using money in the treasury intended for the navy. This depletion of state funds contributes to the defeat of the Chinese in the Sino–Japanese War that same year.

63 YEARS OLD (1898)   After the Hundred Days Reform initiated by Emperor Guangxu fails, he is put under house arrest. Cixi re-takes control of the country.

65 YEARS OLD (1900)   The Boxer Rebellion, an uprising opposed to foreign intervention in China, leads to an invasion by the forces of the Eight–Nation Alliance (the United Kingdom, Russia, Japan, France, the United States of America, Germany, Italy, and Austria-Hungary). Taking the emperor with her, Cixi flees to Xi'an.

This is the greatest number of characters used for an empress's posthumous title of respect in the history of China. It combines all of the honorific names Cixi received in her lifetime and after her death.

孝欽慈禧端佑康頤昭豫莊誠壽恭欽獻崇熙配天興聖顯皇后

66 YEARS OLD (1901)   After signing a punishing peace agreement with the Eight–Nation Alliance, Cixi and Emperor Guangxu return to Beijing.

STARTING AT THE AGE OF 26, I RULED CHINA FOR 47 YEARS!

72 YEARS OLD (1908)   Cixi dies the day after Emperor Guangxu. Puyi, Cixi's handpicked successor, becomes emperor.

THE EMPRESS DOWAGER IS CELEBRATING HER BIG BIRTHDAY

The day Cixi entered the palace was the day she began her lifelong ties with the Palace of Gathered Elegance. She was selected as one of the low-ranking court ladies, but shortly after she entered the palace, she won over the affection of Emperor Xianfeng. He promoted her to the position of Noble Lady and moved her residence to the Palace of Gathered Elegance. It was here that she gave birth to the future Emperor Tongzhi. After becoming an Empress Dowager, Cixi primarily lived in the Palace of Eternal Spring.

On her 50th birthday, Cixi moved back to the Palace of Gathered Elegance. She ordered that the palace be combined with the Palace of Earthly Honor, forming one grand palace that was 102 meters long and 50 meters wide. This was where she planned on enjoying her twilight years.

The cost of this work was 630,000 silver taels. Inside the palace there were about 60 service staff at her command. Cixi lived here for 10 years, in what must have seemed like one long birthday party. On her 60th birthday, she and the party moved to the Hall of Joyful Longevity in the Palace of Tranquil Longevity, where there was an especially gorgeous garden that had been built years before by Emperor Qianlong.

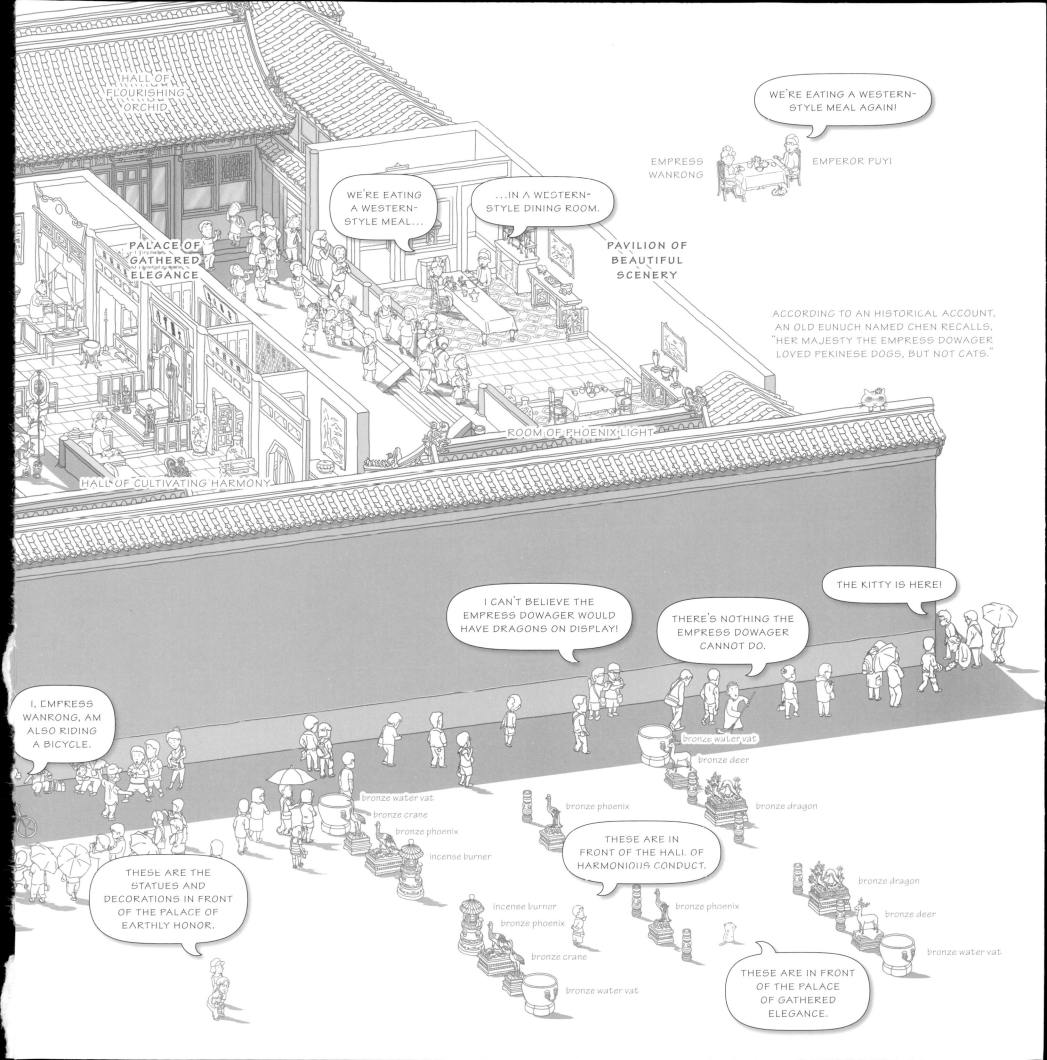

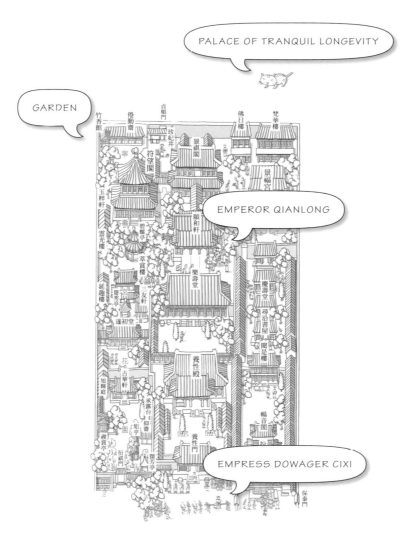

The Garden of the Palace of Tranquil Longevity, also commonly known as the Qianlong Garden, is a narrow but long rectangular area located to the west of the Palace of Tranquil Longevity. It is only 37 meters wide, but 160 meters long. Because it is squeezed in between palaces to the east and a tall wall to the west, this narrow and gloomy space seemed none too ideal for a garden. Yet it is due to these very characteristics that the completed garden owes its singular appearance.

Emperor Qianlong started the trend of Manchu emperors adapting to Han Chinese culture. He personally oversaw the garden's creation, and his influence by traditional Han culture can be detected in every corner, from the overall design to the names of individual places.

Before the completion of the garden the emperor conducted four imperial inspection tours to Jiangnan, the region south of the Yangtze River, where well-known cities such as Nanjing, Suzhou, and Hangzhou are located. His impressions formed by the beautiful scenery of Jiangnan became the primary inspiration for the Garden of Tranquil Longevity.

Limited in size, the garden reflects Qianlong's brilliance in how he recreated a small section of his kingdom in a corner of the Forbidden City.

In 1771, as China was in a prosperous period, the 60-year-old emperor had time to participate in the design of the garden himself, the construction of which was inspired by his life experiences. He had promised to himself and the country that he would pass the throne to his son (the future Emperor Jiaqing) if he reached the 60th year of his reign. This was Qianlong's way of showing the utmost respect to his grandfather, Emperor Kangxi, by not exceeding the 61 years he had been on the throne.

The Palace of Tranquil Longevity was the place Qianlong chose to spend his years after retirement. The Garden of Tranquil Longevity, completed in 1776, reached an unsurpassed height in architectural design and construction, the finest of all the Qing dynasty imperial gardens.

Here is an interesting tidbit. There was another big event that happened in 1776, the same year that the beautiful garden was completed, and it was the creation of a new country – the United States of America.

SO MAGNIFICENT!

EMPEROR QIANLONG'S GRAND DESIGN

In order to counteract the effect of the narrow and lackluster space of the garden, where the palaces press against one side and a high wall constrains the other, Emperor Qianlong devised a system known as "pitting limitation against limitation." He subdivided the space into four courtyards using a great amount of rockery and pavilions as separators. These features are so jam-packed that they create the feeling of walking on rocky mountain paths. The idea behind Qianlong's system is that the more densely packed a space, the more that space will stimulate the imagination. This is known in Chinese as creating "a universe in a pot."

The eight-meter-high wall to the west is set off against the rockery and pavilions, serving as a blank canvas that helps to create a dynamic sense of space. Qianlong was a man steeped in poetry and painting, a great aficionado of high culture. His passions for art and life permeate all corners of the four courtyards.

THE 4TH COURTYARD

But I, as an emperor, still need to project some power and grandeur.

THE 3RD COURTYARD

I want to look at the fine mountains and delicate rivers I have loved all my life.

THE 2ND COURTYARD

All I yearn for is a plain and quiet existence.

THE 1ST COURTYARD

I am a cultivated man.

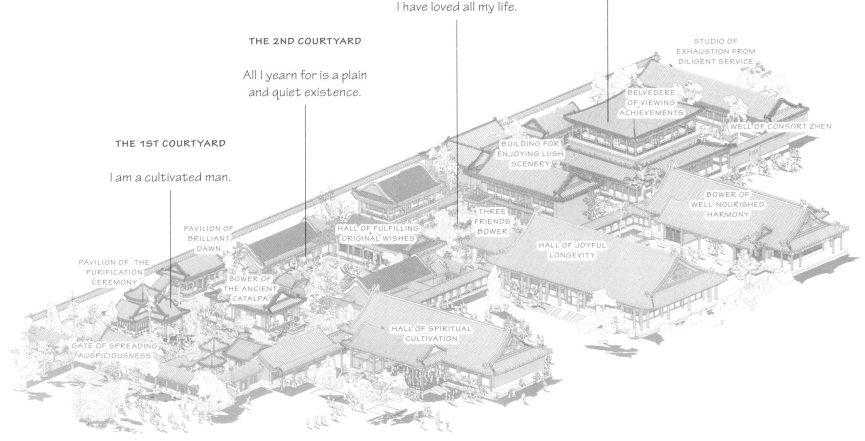

STUDIO OF EXHAUSTION FROM DILIGENT SERVICE

BELVEDERE OF VIEWING ACHIEVEMENTS

WELL OF CONSORT ZHEN

BUILDING FOR ENJOYING LUSH SCENERY

BOWER OF WELL-NOURISHED HARMONY

PAVILION OF BRILLIANT DAWN

HALL OF FULFILLING ORIGINAL WISHES

THREE FRIENDS BOWER

HALL OF JOYFUL LONGEVITY

PAVILION OF THE PURIFICATION CEREMONY

BOWER OF THE ANCIENT CATALPA

HALL OF SPIRITUAL CULTIVATION

GATE OF SPREADING AUSPICIOUSNESS

THE 1ST COURTYARD: THE RECLUSIVE EMPEROR

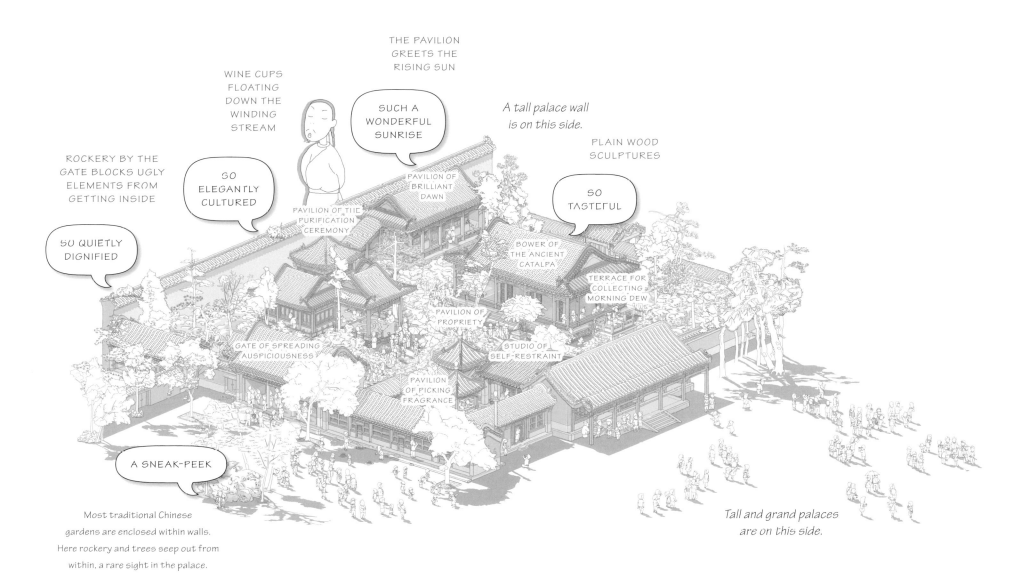

Most traditional Chinese gardens are enclosed within walls. Here rockery and trees seep out from within, a rare sight in the palace.

Tall and grand palaces are on this side.

Entering the garden through the Gate of Spreading Auspiciousness one sees an enormous rockery formation. The rocks form a narrow path, which then opens up to an airy courtyard.

The Pavilion of the Purification Ceremony and the Bower of the Ancient Catalpa are the key structures in the first courtyard. The former was inspired by the Orchid Pavilion Gathering, a famous event where men of letters gathered and wrote poetry in the fourth century. The latter was built around an ancient catalpa tree.

THE 2ND COURTYARD: LETTING GO OF WORLDLY CONCERNS

Entered through the Floral Pendant Gate, the second courtyard is built with common blue bricks, which gives it the humble feel of an ordinary house.

In ancient China, people believed that a house should be built to "embrace the yang and face away from the yin." As a part of this idea, it was believed that the ideal home should have water in front of it and a hill or mountain behind it. So, since there is flowing water in front of the second courtyard, there should be a mountain in the back…

THE 3RD COURTYARD: REMEMBERING JIANGNAN

…And sure enough the focus of the third courtyard is on mountains. Inspired by the magnificent sights of Jiangnan, the region to the immediate south of the Yangtze River, Emperor Qianlong ordered that the mountains be replicated for his enjoyment. The new, smaller versions of these mountains were very expensive. He even had tunnels built inside the hills so that visitors could make-believe that they had stumbled upon the "The Peach Blossom Spring," a secret paradise featured in a famous story.

The Three Friends Bower is ingenuously decorated entirely with pine trees, bamboo, and plum. These plants are called the "Three Friends of Winter," favored for their beauty as well as their tenacity against harsh weather, and are well-known symbols in Chinese art.

THE 4TH COURTYARD: AFTER ALL, THE EMPEROR IS STILL AN EMPEROR

PAVILION OF JADE-GREEN CONCH

The Pavilion of Jade-Green Conch is located on a small rockery hill facing the Belvedere of Viewing Achievements. Separated into five sections and decorated with plum blossoms, it is also known as the Pavilion of Jade-Green Conch and Plum Blossoms. Years earlier, when Emperor Kangxi, grandfather of Qianlong, made his inspection tour to Jiangnan, he liked a certain tea from the region and gave it a special name, "Jade Snail Spring." Emperor Qianlong named this pavilion after fond memories of his grandfather as well as the tea. In December of every year, Emperor Qianlong would give a royal banquet at the Belvedere of Viewing Achievements. The party guests would look at the Pavilion of Jade-Green Conch. Its lively colors and decorations of plum blossoms would remind them that spring was on the way.

Architectural experts have remarked that the placement of the fourth courtyard is Emperor Qianlong's stroke of genius. It is not aligned along the same axis as the other courtyards, which are characterized by their poetic sentiments, monastic simplicity, and intricate landscapes. Here these characteristics are abandoned in favor of a grand structure that evokes the power of the emperor.

The Belvedere of Viewing Achievements, built in 1772, was erected to face the Belvedere of Prolonged Spring to its west, which was built in 1742. Like two invincible warriors guarding the north wall of the Forbidden City, the soaring towers are both Qianlong's masterpieces. Scanning from the east to the west, one takes in 30 years of splendor.

ON THE CENTRAL AXIS: THE IMPERIAL GARDEN

Toward the Six Western Palaces

STUDIO OF SPIRITUAL CULTIVATION

WEST IMPERIAL GARDEN GATE

OFFICE OF THE IMPERIAL PHYSICIANS

STUDIO OF QUIETUDE AND REPOSE

Toward the Three Back Palaces

Right behind the Three Back Palaces is the Imperial Garden, the largest and most distinguished garden inside the Forbidden City. It runs 80 meters from the north to the south and 140 meters from the west to the east, taking up an area of 12,000 square meters.

The garden is located on the sacred central axis of the Forbidden City and its design was restrained by rules governing its use for social and family purposes. There had to be a balance both in the layout of the space and in the ways in which the garden was used. The Imperial Garden was a place where the emperor and his empress and consorts enjoyed leisurely strolls, played, exercised, read books, and occasionally conducted religious ceremonies.

These many uses created a challenge for the garden's designers. They had to create a natural space for enjoyment, but it had to be set against the seriousness of the palaces. In reality all the gardens in the Forbidden City were restricted by space and had to be man-made. For the imperial family, their "real" imperial gardens would have been at the Summer Palace, Yuanmingyuan (the Old Summer Palace), and the Mountain Resort in Chengde, which were 240, 290, and 470 times larger than the Imperial Garden inside the Forbidden City.

In the garden, about 20 buildings are arranged symmetrically on the east and west sides of the Central Axis. For example, the Pavilion of Ten Thousand Springs is across from the Pavilion of a Thousand Autumns and the Pavilion of Floating Jade faces the Pavilion of Purified Auspiciousness. Near the back wall, the Imperial Prospect Pavilion and the Pavilion of Prolonging Splendor echo each other with their grand heights. The central building of the Pavilion of Crimson Snow, which is on the east side of the garden, extends outwards and could be inserted like a puzzle piece in the space between the two wings of the Studio of Spiritual Cultivation – a playful variation within the garden's symmetrical design.

These architectural elements all serve to emphasize the grandeur of the Hall of Imperial Peace, which is located right on the Forbidden City's Central Axis. This hall functioned as a ceremonial altar for the mythological god Xuan Wu. The Imperial Garden was overflowing with exotic decorations and pavilions because the imperial family loved to collect things. All of this was here to serve one person: the Emperor.

STUDIO OF CLEANSING
FRAGRANCE

JADE
PAVILION

STUDIO OF
ESTABLISHING
TEACHINGS

PAVILION OF PURIFIED
AUSPICIOUSNESS

PAVILION OF
A THOUSAND
AUTUMNS

SHRINE OF THE
FOUR DEITIES

GATE OF
HEAVENLY
UNITY

GATE OF EARTHLY
TRANQUILITY

On the garden's winding paths, more than 900 pictures and illustrations were created using tiny colored stones, like a mosaic.

Along these paths, there are many ancient trees. More than 70 are over 100 years old; around 50 of them are more than 300 years old.

Peonies, which symbolize wealth, and potted orchids are the most common flowers in the garden.

Emperor Xianfeng, who had poor health, used to practice sword fighting in this garden.

During the reign of Emperor Jiaqing they would keep deer in the garden to hear them twitter and raise cranes to watch them strut around.

Emperor Daoguang selected his imperial consorts here.

During the Qing dynasty, there were normally 26 eunuchs tasked with doing miscellaneous chores and keeping watch over the garden at night.

Another 15 eunuchs in the garden served as Daoist monks, in charge of incense and religious practices.

Emperor Puyi and his brother Pujie had their picture taken in front of two famous interlocking cypress trees in the garden.

Emperor Puyi assigned one of the garden pavilions to his Scottish tutor Sir Reginald Johnston, for use as a study and residence.

The famous Indian poet Tagore visited the garden in 1924, when he was 63 years old.

There are more than 40 garden landscapes here, which were made using unusually shaped rocks from Lake Tai in the south. The largest rocky landscape is the size of a small hill.

On the 9th day of the 9th lunar month of every year, the emperor, empress, and imperial consorts would climb up the Hill of Accumulated Elegance for the Double Ninth Festival, which is often celebrated by hiking up mountains.

A story goes that Imperial Consort Jin (the elder sister of the ill-fated Imperial Consort Zhen) purchased a mansion for her parents to the east of Jing Mountain, outside the Forbidden City. Almost every night, at twilight, she would ascend the Hill of Accumulated Elegance. There, with the aid of binoculars, she would gaze at her mother standing in the mansion and her mother would gaze back at her. This daily ritual continued until her death in 1924.

All these events are now nothing but tales, idly told among the tourists.

One More Tale: How Puyi, the Last Emperor, Paraded Through the Imperial Garden

Whenever I went for a stroll in the garden a procession had to be organized. In front went a eunuch from the Administrative Bureau [Office of Respectful Service], whose function was roughly that of a motor horn: he walked twenty or thirty yards ahead of the rest of the party intoning the sound "chir… chir…" as a warning to anyone who might be in the vicinity to go away at once. Next came two chief eunuchs advancing [very slowly] on either side of the path; ten paces behind them came the center of the procession – the Empress Dowager or myself. If I was being carried in a chair there would be two junior eunuchs walking beside me to attend to my wants at any moment; if I was walking they would be supporting me. Next came a eunuch with a large silk canopy followed by a large group of eunuchs of whom some were empty-handed and others were holding all sorts of things: a seat in case I wanted to rest, changes of clothing, umbrellas, and parasols. After these eunuchs of the imperial presence came eunuchs of the imperial tea bureau with boxes of various kinds of cakes and delicacies, and, of course, jugs of hot water and a tea service; they were followed by eunuchs of the imperial dispensary carrying cases of medicine and first-aid equipment suspended from carrying poles. The medicines carried always included potions prepared from lampwick sedge, chrysanthemums, the roots of reeds, bamboo leaves, and bamboo skins; in summer there were always Essence of Betony Pills for Rectifying the Vapor, Six Harmony Pills for Stabilizing the Center, Gold Coated Heat-Dispersing Cinnabar, Fragrant Herb Pills, Omnipurpose Bars, colic medicine, and anti-plague powder; and throughout all four seasons there would be the Three Immortals Beverage to aid the digestion, as well as many other medicaments. At the end of the procession came the eunuchs who carried commodes and chamber-pots. If I was walking, a sedan chair, open or covered according to the season, would bring up the rear.

(Excerpt from *From Emperor to Citizen: The Autobiography of Aisin-Gioro Pu Yi*)

PAVILION OF
PROLONGING
SPLENDOR

To the Gate of
Divine Prowess

GATE OF
COLLECTING
HAPPINESS

GATE OF
OBEDIENCE
AND LOYALTY

IMPERIAL
PROSPECT
PAVILION

GATE OF
RECEIVING
LIGHT

HALL OF
IMPERIAL
PEACE

GATE OF
LASTING
PEACE

HILL OF
ACCUMULATED
ELEGANCE

HALL OF
ORNATE
WRITING

PAVILION OF
CONCENTRATED
FRAGRANCE

PAVILION OF
FLOATING JADE

PAVILION OF
TEN THOUSAND
SPRINGS

LODGE OF
FULFILLED
WISHES

PAVILION OF
CRIMSON SNOW

NORTH GATE OF THE FORBIDDEN CITY

The Gate of Divine Prowess is located at the north end of the Forbidden City, 961 meters away from the Meridian Gate. There is a Chinese saying, "The gate of the palace opens to a place as deep as the sea." This not only refers to the vast area of a palace; it also refers to the vast system of laws and regulations contained within. There were different rules for different people, determined by their rank, gender, and whether they lived or served in the Inner Court or the Outer Court. This system was created to agree with rules of etiquette, the imperial power structure, and palace regulations. During the Ming and Qing dynasties, not one person – not even the emperor – was permitted to walk the entire 961-meter distance freely.

There were even rules for the names of places. The Gate of Divine Prowess had been called the Xuan Wu Gate during the Ming dynasty, named after the mythological god that they prayed to in the Hall of Imperial Peace in the Imperial Garden. After the Qing dynasty was founded, there was a rule against using the personal name of emperors. Because the personal name of Emperor Kangxi was Xuan Ye, the name of the gate was changed to Shen Wu, or the Gate of Divine Prowess.

In the Forbidden City, the Gate of Divine Prowess was second in prominence to the Meridian Gate, but it was the most popular for everyday use. The emperors would pass through it when attending to any activity that was not official business. One day Emperor Jiaqing was returning to the palace from *Yuanmingyuan* (the Old Summer Palace). After entering through the Gate of Divine Prowess a dissident named Chen De jumped out of nowhere and attempted to stab him. His assassination attempt failed, but Jiaqing was horribly shaken. Chen De refused to confess to his crime and he was eventually executed. The exact nature of his plot remains an unsolved mystery of the Forbidden City.

On November 5, 1924, Puyi and his wife Wanrong, the last emperor and empress of the Qing dynasty, were forced to leave the palace by the order of Feng Yuxiang, a powerful warlord during China's Republican Era. At 4:00 p.m. they exited through the Gate of Divine Prowess by automobile.

Since the completion of the Forbidden City in 1420, the imperial families of the Ming and Qing dynasties lived here for 504 years. In China, there is an old saying, "No life force, however forceful, can last more than five centuries." This saying rings partly true, in that while imperial China indeed ran out of its life force, the life force of the Forbidden City has not diminished and endures to this day.

EMPEROR
JIAQING

CHEN DE

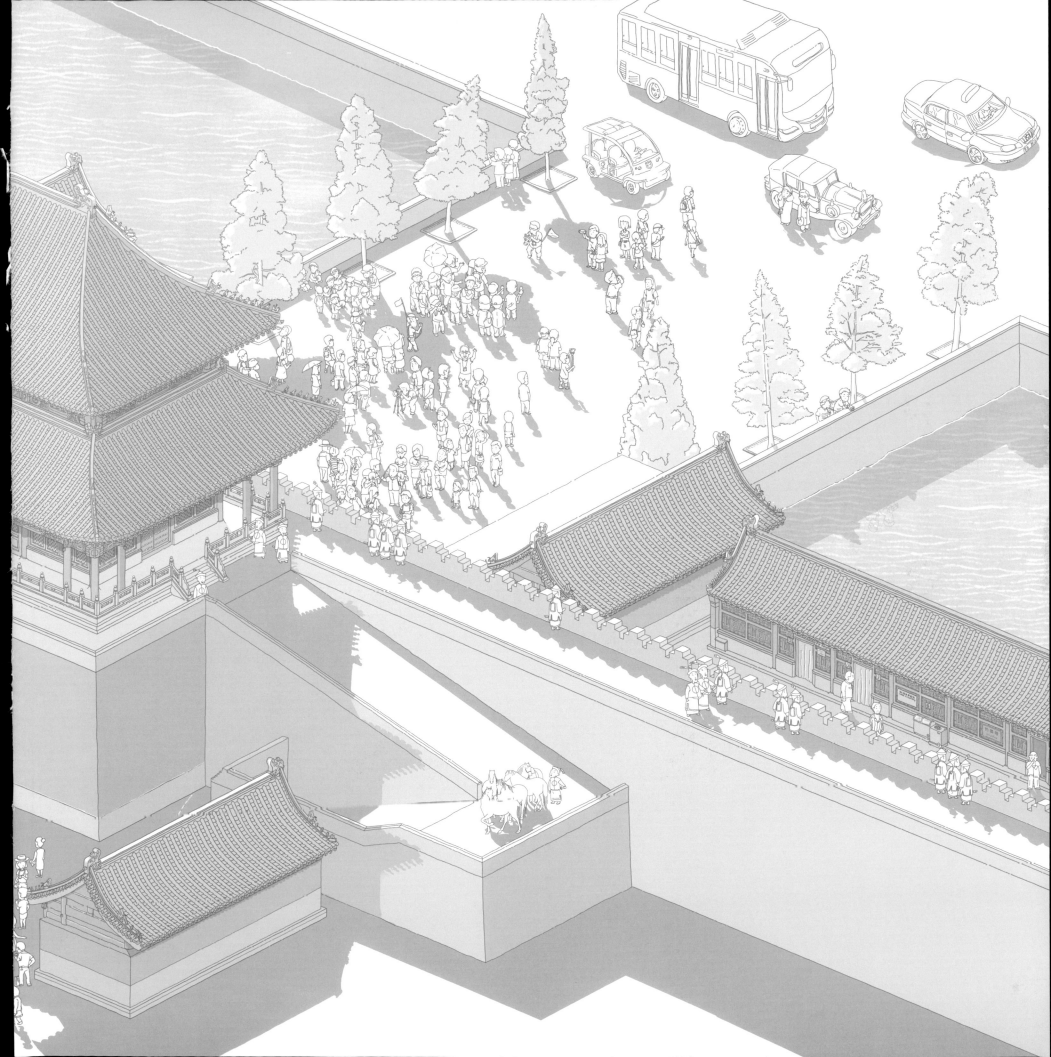

A LETTER FOR YOU, IN THE FUTURE

Hello there, my friends!

As the Forbidden City has been preserved for 600 years, I hope you will also decide to preserve this little book. You can take it out and look at it whenever you want and, when you are older, you can take a look at it once more and remember these stories you read when you were young. Then it will be your turn to think about how you will re-tell these stories to the young children in your life.

Everything in the Forbidden City contains life. However our world has begun to change and become more unreal. The distance between people is greater and greater, the number of animal species is fewer and fewer, and plants are seen more often in parks, photographs, and on digital screens. The adjective "live" will soon need a new definition to be used in lives lived apart from it. So you see, my friends, everything in life deserves contemplation.

We all have something special we treasure. These things could be a story, a memory, or a valuable object. The Forbidden City, which has already been turned into a grand museum, is in itself a huge treasure. It is loaded with the most noteworthy moments of the Ming and Qing dynasties, containing tales and memories that are representative of the Chinese people, and valuable to all of humankind. All this is hidden inside one of the world's greatest palaces.

The truth is, as we are telling you that there were once more than 100,000 people leading their daily lives inside the palace (if the historical records are accurate), we are not completely certain exactly what it must have been like to live there. According to an official report, in 2013 over 175,000 tourists visited the Forbidden City Palace Museum in one day. This number exceeds that of the world's most popular theme parks. For a palace, it is simply incredible.

Most of us will never become an emperor, an empress, a prince, or an imperial minister. It is also difficult for us to imagine life without technology. However, what we do know is that everyone, no matter who they are and which historical period they are from, experiences happiness and unhappiness, and possesses the hope to love and be loved. This hope has been passed on from generation to generation, until it dropped into our hands and we passed it on to you.

Now, my dear friends, we ask that you bring these hopes to the children of tomorrow.

I wish you all the very best!

Chiu Kwong-chiu
Design and Cultural Studies Workshop, Hong Kong

WE ALL LIVE IN THE FORBIDDEN CITY

IN THE FORBIDDEN CITY

Written by Chiu Kwong-chiu
Designed and Illustrated by Design and Cultural Studies Workshop Limited
Translated by Ben Wang
Edited by Nancy S. Steinhardt

Book Design for the English edition by Arthur Gorelik & Design and Cultural Studies Workshop Limited

Managing Editors – Michael Buening and Eva Wen

Copyright © 2014 by China Institute in America

Authorized translation of the English edition © 2014 Design and Cultural Studies Workshop Limited. This translation is published and sold by permission of Design and Cultural Studies Workshop Limited.

Puyi excerpt reprinted from: Aisin-Gioro Pu Yi. *From Emperor to Citizen: The Autobiography of Aisin-Gioro Pu Yi.* Oxford, Great Britain: Oxford University Press, 1987.

Printed in Shenzhen, China by Regent Publishing Services.
First edition, 2014
10 9 8 7 6 5 4 3 2

ISBN 978-0-9893776-0-7

Library of Congress Cataloguing-in-Publication Data is available under

LCCN 2014932006

Distributed by Tuttle Publishing * 364 Innovation Drive, North Clarendon, VT 05759-9436
info@tuttlepublishing.com   www.tuttlepublishing.com

China Institute * 125 East 65th Street, New York, NY 10065-7088
www.chinainstitute.org   www.walfc.org

This book and all *We All Live In The Forbidden City*-related programming has been made possible through the generous support of

何 鴻 毅 家 族 基 金
THE ROBERT H. N. HO
FAMILY FOUNDATION

www.rhfamilyfoundation.org

SPECIAL THANKS

We at China Institute in America wish to express our gratitude to the many people who have worked with us on *In the Forbidden City* and *We All Live in the Forbidden City*. Ted Lipman, Jean Miao, and Wong Mei-yee of the Robert H. N. Ho Family Foundation for their support and guidance in shepherding this project to North America. Chiu Kwong-chiu, Eileen Ng, and Ma Kin-chung of the Design and Cultural Studies Workshop and Alice Mak, Brian Tse and Luk Chi cheong for creating such wonderful books and for their advice and collaboration in developing the English language editions. Wang Yamin of the Palace Museum, and the editorial team of Palace Museum Publishing House, for their vital support and expertise since this program's inception in 2008. We also wish to thank: Qi Yue, Li Ji, and Yang Changqing at the Palace Museum; Christopher Johns at Tuttle Publishing; Lori Takeuchi at the Joan Ganz Cooney Center; Mark Solomon and Alan Chong at Regent Publishing Services; Samuel Ing, Ben Wang, Nancy S. Steinhardt, and Arthur Gorelik.

ABOUT *WE ALL LIVE IN THE FORBIDDEN CITY*

In 2008 The Robert H. N. Ho Family Foundation collaborated with the Design and Cultural Studies Workshop (cnc.org.hk) in Hong Kong to create the *We All Live in the Forbidden City* (fc-edu.org) program. Using a contemporary voice and a variety of media formats, this program celebrates the Forbidden City and the study of architecture, imperial life, and Chinese cultural history in ways that are accessible, appealing, and relevant to children, parents, students, teachers, and the general public.

Working with China Institute in America, this program has now been brought to an English-language audience. Through four books, e-books, education programs, and a website, you will have the opportunity to learn about Chinese culture through this international icon. To learn more about the Forbidden City, WALFC, and to access games, activity guides, and videos, please visit www.walfc.org.

ABOUT CHINA INSTITUTE IN AMERICA

Since its founding in 1926, China Institute has been dedicated to advancing a deeper understanding of China through programs in education, culture, business, and art in the belief that cross-cultural understanding strengthens our global community.

THE NIGHT BEFORE
CHRISTMAS

THE NIGHT BEFORE
CHRISTMAS

THE ANNIVERSARY EDITION

By Clement C. Moore
Illustrated by Christian Birmingham

RP|KIDS
CLASSICS
PHILADELPHIA • LONDON

20 19 18 17 16 15 14 13 12 11
Digit on the right indicates the number of this printing.

Library of Congress Control Number: 95-67238

ISBN 978-0-7624-2416-0

Cover and interior illustrations by Christian Birmingham
Interior design by Frances J. Soo Ping Chow
Typography: Caslon Antique by Justin T. Scott

Printed in China

This book may be ordered by mail from the publisher.
Please include $2.50 for postage and handling.
But try your bookstore first!

Published by Running Press Kids, an imprint of
Running Press Book Publishers
2300 Chestnut Street
Philadelphia, PA 19103-4371

Visit us on the web!
www.runningpress.com

Introduction

In 1822, a New York clergyman named Clement Clarke Moore spun together Christmas memories for his children. The poem he wrote featured a red-suited Santa in a reindeer-drawn sleigh, a never-empty sack of toys, and stockings hung expectantly above the fireplace. He called it *A Visit from St. Nicholas*, and it was then published anonymously in a newspaper in Troy, New York. It captured the public's imagination. The poem's opening line—"'Twas the night before Christmas"—soon replaced the original title.

One reason Moore's poem has endured is that it is a joy to read aloud. Beginning in hushed suspense, the poem builds to a dramatic crescendo as the rollicking verses usher in the mysterious midnight visitor.

A tale of anticipation and wonder, *The Night Before Christmas* has become a holiday tradition in itself for many families. So as you open these pages, whether for a first Christmas or to recall those past, celebrate and share the timeless joys of this enchanting holiday.

'Twas the night before Christmas,

when all through the house

Not a creature was stirring,

not even a mouse;

The stockings were hung

by the chimney with care,

In hopes that St. Nicholas

soon would be there.

The children were nestled

all snug in their beds,

While visions of sugarplums

danced in their heads;

And Mama in her kerchief

and I in my cap,

Had just settled down

for a long winter's nap—

When out on the lawn

there rose such a clatter,

I sprang from my bed

to see what was the matter.

Away to the window

I flew like a flash,

Tore open the shutters

and threw up the sash.

The moon on the breast

of the new-fallen snow,

Gave a luster of midday

to objects below;

When, what to my wondering eyes

should appear,

But a miniature sleigh

and eight tiny reindeer,

With a little old driver

so lively and quick,

I knew in a moment

it must be St. Nick.

More rapid than eagles

his coursers they came,

And he whistled, and shouted,

and called them by name—

"Now, Dasher! Now, Dancer!

Now, Prancer and Vixen!

On, Comet! On, Cupid!

On, Donder and Blitzen!

To the top of the porch,

to the top of the wall!

Now, dash away! Dash away!

Dash away all!"

As dry leaves before

the wild hurricane fly,

When they meet with an obstacle,

mount to the sky,

So up to the housetop

the coursers they flew,

With sleigh full of toys—

and St. Nicholas too;

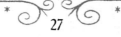

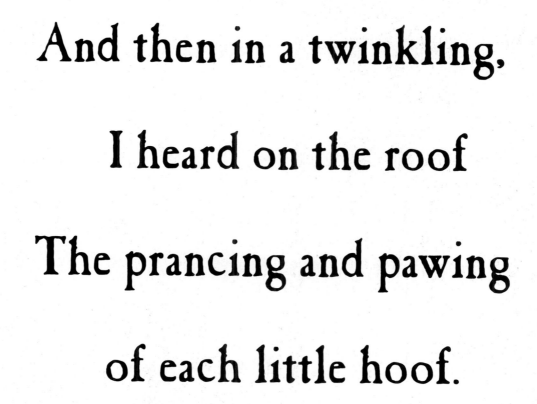

And then in a twinkling,

I heard on the roof

The prancing and pawing

of each little hoof.

As I drew in my head

and was turning around,

Down the chimney St. Nicholas

came with a bound.

He was dressed all in fur

from his head to his foot,

And his clothes were all tarnished

with ashes and soot.

A bundle of toys

he had flung on his back,

And he looked like a peddler

just opening his pack.

His eyes how they twinkled!

His dimples how merry!

His cheeks were like roses,

his nose like a cherry!

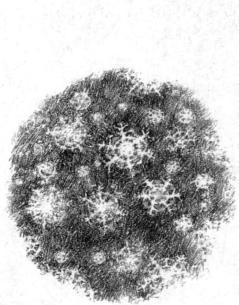

His droll little mouth

was drawn up like a bow,

And the beard on his chin

was as white as the snow!

The stump of a pipe

he held tight in his teeth,

And the smoke it encircled

his head like a wreath.

He had a broad face

and a little round belly

That shook when he laughed

like a bowl full of jelly.

He was chubby and plump—

a right jolly old elf,

And I laughed when I saw him,

in spite of myself.

A wink of his eye

    and a twist of his head,

Soon gave me to know

    I had nothing to dread.

He spoke not a word,

   but went straight to his work,

And filled all the stockings

   then turned with a jerk,

And laying his finger

aside of his nose,

And giving a nod,

up the chimney he rose.

He sprang to his sleigh,

to his team gave a whistle,

And away they all flew

like the down of a thistle.

But I heard him exclaim

as he drove out of sight,

"Merry Christmas to all

and to all a Good Night!"